# The End Is Not the Trophy

# The End Is Not the Trophy

## Reflections on a Life in Coaching

G. David Odom

*With a Foreword by*
Terry Holland

CAROLINA ACADEMIC PRESS
Durham, North Carolina

ISBN 0-89089-881-2
LCCN 97-77216

**Carolina Academic Press**
700 Kent Street
Durham, North Carolina 27701
Telephone (919) 489-7486
Fax (919) 493-5668
www.cap-press.com

Printed in the United States of America

*To my Lynn...Lane and Ryan...with all my love*
*...for a lifetime of memories together.*

I t is not the critic who counts, not the man who points out how the strong man stumbles or where the doer of deeds could have done them better. The credit belongs to the man who is actually in the arena, whose face is marred by dust and sweat and blood, who strives valiantly, who errs and comes up short again and again because there is no effort without error and shortcomings, who knows the great devotion, who spends himself in a worthy cause, who at the best knows in the end the high achievement of triumph and who at worst, if he fails while daring greatly, knows his place shall never be with those timid and cold souls who know neither victory nor defeat.

*— Theodore Roosevelt*

# Contents

# Foreword

Dave Odom's ability as a basketball coach has been recognized in the numerous coaching awards presented by many different organizations. This book gives you an inside look into the reasons for his success in his chosen profession. It goes without saying that Coach Odom has a "passion for the game," but it is a passion born of respect for the history and traditions of this great game, and particularly for that special brand of basketball played on "Tobacco Road."

Dave was an impressionable twelve-year-old self-described sports nut when the ACC was formed in 1954. Therefore, he has been an active spectator and participant in all of the glorious history of ACC basketball. That background makes this story a warm and inspiring account of growing up, under the spell of the excitement and intensity of those early days of ACC basketball, to become the hottest coaching commodity in that storied league.

Dave Odom is as "southern" as Spanish moss. That comes across loud and clear in his writing and should help all basketball fans understand the religious overtones that creep into conversations about college basketball in this part of the country.

It's only fair to point out that I do not pretend to be objective about Dave and his family. It is not coincidental that we graduated in 1960 from high schools about a three-point shot away from each other in eastern North Carolina and that when I had a coaching vacancy in 1982, Dave Odom was the only candidate I considered.

Southerners of our vintage grew up playing in the feather beds of our grandparents' homes. Those feather beds covered the sharp edges of life, but anyone who thinks southerners are ignorant of life's edges has never been to a hog killing or cropped tobacco while visiting those same grandparents. True to his roots, Dave Odom is subtle in exposing the sharp edges of ACC competition but they are there for those who feel beneath the covers.

All in all, this book reminds me of my granny's biscuits— they were a tasty part of the meal itself, but really came in handy to push food on your fork and to "sop" your plate at the end of the meal. Add a little syrup or honey and they became a fine dessert as well. My granny always wanted you to enjoy her cooking and never scolded us when we literally licked our plates clean. I hope you will feel the same way about Dave's book.

*Terry Holland*
*University of Virginia*

# Preface

This book, written about coaches and their families, is for coaches or for anyone, male or female, who has ever thought about coaching as a profession.

Any first-time effort such as this requires a great deal of encouragement from someone who recognizes the need for such an undertaking and is convinced that, if it is done with care, it will make a difference. Dr. Herb Appenzeller, my friend, former football coach, and athletic director emeritus at Guilford suggested that I consider such a project and later provided the motivation to actually begin and complete the work. To him, I will always be indebted.

The professionals at Carolina Academic Press, particularly my editor, Linda Lacy, have been nothing short of terrific. Linda has guided my every step. She understood my varied time constraints, my lack of experience as a writer, and through it all was my primary source of energy, enthusiasm, and encouragement. Without her support and direction, closure of the project would not have been possible.

What would a head coach be without a great staff and supportive players? Truly, I have been blessed each year with both. Without them there would be no stories and no book. I love them all and appreciate their loyalty.

By our own admission, basketball coaches seek to be "Guardians of the Game" and, as such, it is our charge to not only protect, but to contribute to, the overall development of the game and our profession. Though far from perfect, I hope that the thoughts and experiences presented for consideration will prove to be a point of reference for both veteran and young or aspiring coaches. While reading, please remember that the book was not intended to be a blueprint for coaching success, rather it is a compilation of nearly a lifetime of experience gained coaching youngsters at virtually every level.

It is my hope that readers will objectively review each chapter, each anecdote, each experience on its own merit. In coaching, as in life, there is no *one way*. Surely, there are many tried and true methods, but the majesty of coaching is that it is a profession driven by people who care about others. Coaches are highly motivated and success-oriented. They are tireless workers and are forever loyal to their own. But most of all, they are loving givers who care deeply about their colleagues and those whom they coach.

The mystery of coaching is solved when you realize that the way you coach is up to you. Every team and season is different. Every player is different. Thus, it follows that every situation is different and requires that the discerning coach be creative and forthright in his approach. *The End Is Not the Trophy* was written with passion and from the heart, because that is the way I coach.

# The End Is Not the Trophy

# Chapter 1

# Coaching, of Course...
# What Else?

*"I don't remember the first day that I said
I wanted to coach, but I can't ever remember a day
when I wanted to do anything else."*

W hen I was as young as five or six years old, I knew
that I wanted to be a coach. Sports to me was just
something I did. That's what I did when I woke up in the
morning. I grew up just a short bicycle ride away from the
Boy's Club in Goldsboro, North Carolina. You actually
couldn't join the Boy's Club before you were six years old,
but they didn't run me away. I was just there. Early in my
life, sports people let me enter their world.

I had no decisions to make when I woke up in the mornings like other kids. I knew where I was going and I knew
what I was going to do. It was what people I grew up with
did. We were seasonal athletes. We played whatever sport
was in season and the weather dictated what we did. As the
leaves changed, we played football; as the leaves left, we
played basketball; as they came back, we played baseball and
tennis. On rainy days we would play table tennis or chess or
whatever—but it was always play and compete, play and
compete.

Almost everyone I grew up with was interested in athletics, but my devotion to sports was more pronounced than others'. It was what I did.

My early life was molded almost unintentionally by a lot of people—always in the direction of teaching, coaching, and being around athletics or sports. Every sport that I've tried has been easy for me and I've always felt comfortable in each one. That doesn't mean that I was the best player, but understanding each game came naturally.

I don't remember the first day that I said I wanted to coach, but I can't ever remember a day when I wanted to do anything else.

M y dad was a businessman—he was a Pontiac/Cadillac dealer in Goldsboro—and he built the business hoping that one day I would take it over. I think that up until the very end he really hoped his dream would materialize—hoped against hope, probably. If it hadn't been for my mother as a buffer, things might have been hard. Although my dad liked watching me play, clearly he did not consider that work. He couldn't envision anybody getting paid to do something like coaching. He grew up in an era when you worked, and work was work.

My mother, however, understood that there was another side to me and that in order to be successful you've got to be happy. She knew that my happiest moments were times spent on the ball field or on the court or in the game room—anywhere I could actively compete.

As I grew older, it became very clear that I would actually be doing my dad a favor if I *didn't* go into the business, because I'd have played at it. Everything that he had built would probably have deteriorated in very short order. So it worked out better for everyone that I didn't follow that path and, to my dad's credit, he finally let me follow my heart.

In the later stages of my college career it was very obvious that I was not going into business, that I was going to follow the coaching path. I think one of the great lessons that everyone has to learn is to listen to your own heart and pursue your own dreams. It is perhaps even more difficult to accept a son's destiny and help him follow his own path.

My dad did get to the point where he was able to support my choice and even be enthusiastic about it. One of my regrets is that he never saw even my first year of coaching. He died in 1963, while I was still at Guilford College, and never got to see how happy it made me.

I 'm amazed today at the number of problems that players have with coaches and teachers and people in authority. As I look back on my experiences—and maybe I was different—I can honestly say I never had a bad coach or a bad teacher.

Certainly the people, other than my parents, who were the greatest influence on me were my coaches and my teachers. If you were to ask me about my third-grade teacher or my fifth-grade teacher or my English teacher in the eighth grade, I could tell you about every one of them. I could tell you their names and almost the time of day that they taught me. They're indelible in my mind.

Growing up, I took something from every one of them. If you were to ask me about any coach I could tell you exactly what he taught me, even if it was something intangible, or a personal trait, like love or loyalty.

For instance, my junior high football coach was a man named Harvey Davis who later became principal of the school. Coach Davis was the consummate family man who gave a tremendous, tremendous effort and was totally committed to his team. But he, more than any other coach I had, was able to separate his personal life from his duties as a coach. When the practice was over at five o'clock in the afternoon, it was over. Coach Davis became Harvey Davis, the family man. He was able to separate the two arenas. He was a good coach and he knew football, but he was also a good family man and he was never in danger of becoming sick over the game. He was going to take each day as it came.

That's an important lesson, because I think as coaches we get eaten up with, and consumed by, our jobs. If it's not 24-hours-a-day, guilt sets in, and we feel that we are cheating our jobs or we sense others are working and getting ahead of us.

My high school basketball coach, Charles Lee, was a stickler for detail. He was very structured as a coach. He had virtual control of the team from the sideline. My high school baseball coach was very emotional. He felt that energy and enthusiasm and excitement would make up for whatever ability you might lack. So you played harder, and the will to win was more important than execution or sheer athletic ability.

Y oung people today may talk about their coaches being abusive or being lousy role models, but the thing that I remember about my coaches is that they were all good teachers. They took great pride in their classroom work and that carried over to the athletic front. Back in those days, teaching was their main concern. When I was growing up, coaches taught; that's what they did all day long. They taught in the classroom for four or five hours a day and then they went out to the athletic field and they carried that teaching skill and acumen with them. They all had different approaches, but they were all good teachers. They all taught fundamentals and they all left something with me that I can, to this day, cling to.

Every coach I had was different, yet I think that each one was happy doing what he was doing and felt that I would be happy and good at it, too. They encouraged me more by just being who they were than by sitting me down and saying, "Son, you ought to be a coach. You'd be very good at it."

They probably knew what I was going to do before my parents knew. Because *they* were happy coaching, they just thought, "What's he going to do?" "Yeah, he's going to coach. What else would he do?"

I think even my teachers who weren't coaches knew what I was going to do. I had a certain English teacher for four years who moved up every year I moved up. I often see her when I go back to Goldsboro—she was probably my favorite teacher. Although I was not her best student, I think I was probably her favorite student because she sensed that I knew what I was going to do with my life, and in her way, she was always a positive influence on my life.

I chose Guilford College in Greensboro, NC because it was an easy choice for a kid growing up in Goldsboro. A lot of people from Goldsboro went to Guilford. There's a large Quaker contingent there and the chairman of the Guilford Board of Trustees at that time was from Goldsboro, so it was an easy decision to make.

A small school gave me the opportunity to continue what I had already started. For instance, I was able to play more than one sport. A large university would have required a lot more specialization and probably would not have afforded me the diverse sports opportunities that Guilford gave me. Because I grew up in a one-school town, going from a small, eastern North Carolina town to a small college was easy for me socially. A small college setting was right for me and Guilford was the right small school. It was the college whose time had come for me. I had no problem adjusting.

The first year I played football, basketball, and baseball. After that year I stopped playing baseball because it interfered with basketball and spring football, but I continued to play football and basketball.

I got my first taste of coaching during my college summers. I would go back home each summer and work with the Boy's Club in various camp settings, a job I enjoyed. In terms of actually coaching during the school year, my time was taken up with my own personal play. I didn't, for instance, go down to the Greensboro YMCA and coach during basketball season. There just wasn't time.

My last semester at Guilford I did my student teaching. I was responsible for several health and physical education classes, but I also helped as a student assistant coach with the after-school sports programs. The emphasis was more on formal classroom time, however.

Milton Reese was my student teaching supervisor at Aycock Junior High School in Greensboro. He was an excellent teacher who coached all three sports. He really helped me along, and my student teaching experience confirmed what I knew I wanted to do all along. I enjoyed the experience and enjoyed working with the students but, for the first time, I began to see the kids in a different light. I had crossed the line between being an active player and being a coach.

I never had problems knowing what I wanted to do after college or preparing to do it. I have problems today understanding kids that don't know what they want to do. At some point choosing a profession is a lot like choosing a wife or a husband for life. When you see her or him, you *know*. There's not any, "Do I want to marry him?" "Do I want to marry her?" I guess maybe I grew up in a simpler age; such things just seemed to happen naturally. When I graduated from Guilford in 1965, I remember saying to Lynn, "Listen, I've taken a job in Goldsboro teaching and coaching. I want to get married so we can be together. We did, and I don't think that either one of us has ever regretted that decision which we made together.

A fter college, my first job was back in Goldsboro, where I coached and taught high school for four years. It was rather odd, going back to my hometown. Everyone looked at me a little differently. The snotty-nosed kid everyone had seen riding his bike and showing up everywhere was suddenly a teacher and in a position of some authority.

It wasn't too hard, though, because I didn't worry about it. I think I've always been fairly perceptive. I understand the way people think, but I also understand that there are certain things that you can't do anything about, and you just move on. I really worked at being a good teacher and a good coach. The hardest thing was stepping over the line from being one of the community, one of the guys, to being a coach.

In Goldsboro, I had classroom teaching duties as well as athletic duties. I had a degree and teaching certification that allowed me to teach almost everything. The only thing I didn't feel comfortable teaching was science. Social studies, humanities, physical education, health, driver's education — I taught them all at some point. But I was fortunate that I was not overloaded any one year with, say, five book subjects, plus the coaching. My principals all had compassion for me. They knew coaches needed some time during the day to plan and prepare for our after-school duties.

At that point, I was a varsity assistant coach in football, basketball, and baseball. In truth, I felt as comfortable in one as I did in the other. I still hold to the claim that today I could just as easily be coaching football or baseball as basketball. At that point, I had spent an equal amount of time on each and felt very comfortable in each one of those sports.

The reason I'm in basketball today is because that's where the first opening came. Basketball offered me the first opportunity to be a head coach and I've followed that path ever since. I think that once you get into a track, you're kind of harnessed in that area. You get categorized; you get labeled: "He's a basketball coach." "He's a football coach." "He's a baseball coach." It's difficult to change that perception. It may even be unwise to change tracks because you would have to backpedal and start over again. And so basketball came first.

In all honesty, I think basketball was best for me because there are so many football coaches, and high school and college baseball always seem to be reacting to professional baseball.

I n many ways, my high school coaching years were my happiest years. Relationships that I had with the faculty—particularly the coaches that I worked with on a day-to-day basis—were certainly unique. We were extremely close. We did everything together. Our families, at times, lived as one. We worked hard, we practiced hard, and we coached hard, yet there was down time when we could have outdoor cookouts, or go to a movie, or even take a vacation together.

They were important days, too, because socially, the years that I coached high school were turbulent years in our communities and our schools. Our schools were under court order to integrate, and emotions ran hot. Each day was a challenge, but they were important days, because looking back 25 years later, you realize, "Hey, we did make an impact and some things are better now." And we got through some troubled times. We had kids who had grown up in towns across the South thinking from the day they were five years old—and old enough to know the difference—that they were going to a certain high school. And suddenly, everything changed.

Those years were truly some of my most satisfying years as a coach. Occasionally, I run into one of my former players, and knowing that I had the opportunity to positively affect his life, to me, makes it all worthwhile.

B eing able to coach several different sports gives you a greater appreciation for young people's lives and the time demands on them. At the high school level and below, we should encourage kids to diversify themselves, to experience as many sports as possible. As a youngster, I found that I had a different set of friends in almost each sport that I played and that was quite healthy.

That was also true as a high school coach. I coached all three seasons — most of the sports at one time or another — and I had different kinds of kids playing each sport. It really gave me a chance to broaden my experiences and appreciate the differences in kids.

Unless a youngster is extremely gifted in a given sport, we as educators — as teachers and as coaches — should encourage them to play all sports and not specialize too soon. I think that, in general, early specialization is wrong and in some ways proves to be nothing more than fool's gold.

As a player, I had been seasonal. I felt comfortable in each sport. The positions that I played were positions of leadership — quarterback in football, second base in baseball, guard in basketball. That was always what I did. It was never a matter of who the leader of the team was — it was me. It was easy for me. Growing up, I had been taught to assume that role — by the folks at the Boy's Club and by my different coaches and other people of influence in my life.

I do think that there's an easy crossover from one sport to the other. No matter what the sport, you're still dealing with the psychology of people, the psychology of sport, the psychology of motivating and teaching. The rules of the games change, but the way you motivate people remains basically the same. Perhaps the level at which you coach will dictate some of your methods of leadership. But natural is always better.

A fter four years of coaching at Goldsboro High School (two years as head basketball coach), I moved to Durham as the head basketball coach at Durham High School. I was twenty-six years old. I taught two classes of history and a couple of driver's education classes. One year, our football coach, Kelly Minyard, quit right before the season started, so I took over football that year. I also coached tennis for a while. I still play tennis a lot and, actually, that probably could have been my best sport.

Eventually I became the athletic coordinator at Durham High. As athletic coordinator, you have a tendency to be interested in all of the sports and how they are developing. At the time, I had no idea that the athletes I coached then would continue to have such an impact on my life. One of my real joys is hearing from former players who have become adults with their own families and their own interests. Many have done quite well, but there are some who never quite found themselves.

For instance, I am in monthly contact with a former manager of mine who was accused and eventually convicted of murder. He has spent the last nine years in prison, and we are hopeful that he will be paroled soon and will eventually find his way back into society and become a productive citizen.

D uring the years I coached at Durham High School we won several district and sectional championships and made it deep into state championship play. Those were really important years for me. The Durham experience was particularly important to me because it was where, as I got older, I began to make different friends. I realized that the closest friends a coach could have were other coaches. My interest in college coaching grew at that point because I was literally only four miles away from Cameron Indoor Stadium at Duke. I was about eleven miles from Chapel Hill, twenty-seven miles from North Carolina State and about seventy-five miles from Wake Forest.

I could practice basketball with my team on Saturday morning from nine o'clock to eleven-thirty, go home, shower, have a quick bite to eat, leave my house at twelve-forty, and be at Cameron Indoor Stadium for a Duke–Carolina game at one o'clock with no problem.

When I went to the Duke games, if I didn't have a regular ticket, I would just go to the back door and the concession guy would wave me in. Those were important years because I began to watch college basketball and got to know people like Vic Bubas, Bucky Waters, Chuck Daly, Hubie Brown, Tony Barone, and Neill McGeachy.

All of those people were part of the Duke basketball scene at the time, and they took me into their circle, if only on an unofficial level, and exposed me to their lives. I began to see what a life of travel, recruiting, coaching, dealing with the media, and representing a university would be like. It was an important time for me.

Yet nothing will surpass the experience that I had coaching at the high school level. I was only twenty-six years old when I became a head coach and to be at a place like Durham High School and be able to work for a man like Paul Williamson was an experience I will never forget.

The early seventies, when desegregation really hit us all, were trying times, and yet very, very important days in all of our lives. To work together as a school system, as a faculty, as a community—to see that unfold and to come out of it okay—was pretty special.

T he jump from high school to college coaching didn't seem unusual at the time, but now it's a much more difficult transition to make. I was always quietly confident that I would eventually coach at the collegiate level. The fact that high school coaches almost never made it to the college level made no difference to me. I was different—and opportunity found me.

Y ears ago, back in the mid-'70s or the early '80s, the summer sports camps as we know them today were almost nonexistent. However, there were a few, and the most famous camp at that time was a privately owned camp called the Five-Star Basketball Camp.

I was at Durham High at the time and Chuck Daly was an assistant basketball coach at Duke. (Daly went on to win back-to-back NBA titles in 1989 and 1990 as head coach of the Detroit Pistons, and to be the 1992 Olympic head coach of the gold medal-winning "Dream Team." He is currently the head coach of the Orlando Magic.) I went out to Duke all the time and played tennis with their coaching staff and attended their games. Durham was a great place to live if you were a high school coach because you could go to all of the college games and still coach your own team.

Chuck Daly said to me one time, "I teach at the Five-Star Basketball Camp in the summertime. You should think about working the camp. Would you be interested?" And I said, "Absolutely. Tell me about it."

In the Pocono Mountains of Pennsylvania every summer for two weeks, one in June and one in August, many of the best high school players in the country would learn the game from the game's best teachers (Hubie Brown, Bob Knight, Rick Pitino, Mike Fratello and others) while they developed their skills under the watchful eye of America's top college coaches. The nation's best college players would go up into the Poconos in the summer and work at the area's resort hotels by day and play ball at night with players from New York City—kids like John Roche (South Carolina), Lenny Rosenbluth (UNC), and Art Heyman (Duke).

The camp, and the basketball played around the hotels, made a visit to the Poconos a must for every aspiring coach. So Chuck Daly said to me, "I'll have the co-director of the camp, Mr. Garfinkel, call you." And I thought, "Won't ever happen."

But one day in March as I was sitting at my desk at Durham High, Howard Garfinkel called me and mentioned that he'd think about hiring me. He had never hired a southern coach before, and he was somewhat apprehensive about it.

I said that I'd really like to go that summer but he said, "I can't do it this summer. My staff is full. But next summer I'll call you back if you're really interested." I said fine, and I thought, "Won't ever hear," but I did. "Garf" called in January of the following year and the rest is history.

I had a good team coming back to Durham High and arranged for those players to go to the camp as well. For me, it was a door of opportunity that opened right before my eyes. It wasn't because of anything I had done; it was because of people that I knew, who I had been exposed to. Both Chuck Daly and Hubie Brown, who was another assistant at Duke at that time, were involved in the camp. (Hubie Brown went on to be an NBA head coach with the Atlanta Hawks, where he was NBA Coach of the Year in 1978, and with the New York Knicks. For many years he has been a successful television basketball analyst.) Through their kindness, they got me involved with Garf and Will Klein, his partner.

Here was a Jewish guy in New York who had never hired a southern coach before and who didn't know me and didn't have to take an interest, but he did, he really cared. He wanted to expand and he wanted good teachers.

So I went up there for a couple of years and carved myself a southern niche. I was the only southerner there. I talked funny and I was kind of an enigma to the staff. I was different, and everyone seemed to enjoy the differences.

I'll never forget the day that I was teaching the pick and roll at my station, and I heard Garfinkel talking right outside the fence. He said, "I discovered this guy here. He's going to be a great coach one day." I looked around and he was talking to Joe Hall, who was the head coach at Kentucky at the time. I realized it was me they were watching and talking about. I thought to myself, "Wow, how lucky can you be. I mean, you're right here." It really motivated me to continue.

Another one of the camps I worked every summer was the Wake Forest camp. I had worked there two straight summers after Carl Tacy was named head coach. I was now firmly entrenched in the Five-Star Camp and all of these great players were coming through the camp and I had a natural entree to them. Young players such as Sam Bowie, Michael Jordan, Jeff Lamp, Isiah Thomas, and Dominique Wilkins all passed through the Five-Star Camp during my time as a camp coach.

I think Coach Tacy looked at the situation and thought, "He knows North Carolina, he's familiar with the ACC, and he's also got connections to these great players that are coming through the Five-Star Camp. Maybe he could get some of these players for Wake Forest." At that time, it was legal for me to work the camp and still be a college coach. So that's how it happened. He had an opening on his staff and offered me the job and I took it.

I may have become a college coach in time, but there's no question in my mind that the camp and the friendships I made with Garf and his staff proved invaluable to me as a young aspiring coach.

M y first year at Wake Forest proved to be particularly satisfying. We had a veteran team returning, and the team made its way all the way to the "Elite Eight" in the country, only to lose to the eventual national champions, Marquette University, coached by Al McGuire.

We had a great team with Skip Brown and Frank Johnson as our guards, a tall center in Larry Harrison, and a great shooter in Jerry Schellenberg. The catalyst for our team, however, was Rod Griffin, who was named ACC Player of the Year for the 1976–77 season.

Our next two years, though not as productive from a won/lost standpoint, were important because we recruited very well, and the foundation for later Wake Forest teams was built during those years. I was at Wake Forest for three years, and was then offered the head coaching job at East Carolina University in Greenville, North Carolina, where I stayed for three years.

I had been on the job at East Carolina less than a week when I went to my first booster club meeting, a meeting of the Pirate Club.

The executive director of the ECU Pirate Club, who is a wonderful man and ended up being one of my best friends and one of my best supporters, invited me to come up to a fundraiser in Raleigh. He said that Coach Pat Dye—who was at the height of his football career at East Carolina—

was going to be there and I'd get a chance to meet a lot of people. I thought it was a great opportunity for me and so made the trip up to Raleigh.

There were several hundred people in the audience that night and the athletic director got up and said that he was pleased to see everybody and went on to say, "I know you were expecting Coach Dye to be here but something happened at the last minute and he wasn't able to come. However, we do have our new basketball coach here and if you would give him a big Pirate welcome that would be great."

It was almost as if basketball was an afterthought. I don't think it was meant that way, but things like that subtly stick in your mind. I was coming off a Wake Forest experience where basketball was very important, and to hear the AD say that football was our flagship sport, and always would be, was hard for me. There's nothing wrong with that, but I can't say that I went into the situation with my eyes open.

Although some really good things happened during the time that I was at East Carolina, there were also things that I realized I could never change. If we had a Saturday night game and were playing William and Mary—an important game for us—our players spent all Saturday afternoon watching ACC basketball on television. You could almost feel them asking, "Why not us? Why can't we be on regional or national TV?" I always felt inadequate because I knew that I could never get them what they wanted or felt they deserved.

T he decision to leave being a head coach at East Carolina to become an assistant again was an easy decision for me. I don't have trouble with decisions. I listen to my heart. The ACC is not just a basketball league, it is the best basketball league in the country.

East Carolina was a valuable three years. But back in the seventies and eighties, and I think to a lesser extent now, East

Carolina thought of itself as a football school. I'd gotten used to Wake Forest where basketball was the most important sport. You arrived at the site of the game, and no matter what gym you went to, it was packed and cameras were churning and the lights were on and it was an event. I missed that at ECU. There was nothing wrong with East Carolina — it was an important time for me — but it's almost like the ocean. . . . Once you've gotten past the ocean's surface and have seen the beauty of the ocean floor and its inhabitants, and you have experienced life where few humans have ever gone, then you can never be satisfied with only the froth of the ocean's waves.

When the opportunity came to go to the University of Virginia, even as an assistant, it wasn't a hard decision. At that time Ralph Sampson was there, and they were ranked number one in the country in the preseason polls. And though I had nothing to do with that, there was an opportunity to be part of a great program and a great university at a special time in its history. You don't have the chance to be part of a national championship chase every year, and Terry Holland, the coach at UVA, was giving me the opportunity. It occurred to me that somebody was going to do it, and it might as well be me. So it wasn't a hard decision for me at all.

M y seven years as an assistant coach at Virginia were dotted with one great memory after another. They were great years. Basketball at the University of Virginia was as important then as it is now and Terry Holland was absolutely the best to work for. He gave you so much leeway and so much freedom. He never said, "This is what I want you to do and this is how I want you to do it." Instead it was, "This is what I want you to do, now develop it. Come back to me if you need some help." He was one of the most benevolent, giving men I have ever been around, yet he was one of the most complex.

C oach Holland always went at problems in different ways. As co-workers we developed what we called a "T" mentality. You would think about something in a rational way, and then you would think about it as Terry might. There was always a different way—and a very good way.

It was interesting how he dealt with the players, how he circled the wagons around Ralph and the team. Terry built a small kingdom there. I don't think he did it intentionally, but it was almost cocoon-like. We were part of the athletic department and part of the university but we were a very important part and there were not many times that we were subjected to busywork or pointless meetings like most of the other coaches in other sports. The financial limitations that strapped other teams didn't affect us.

With that freedom to operate the program came enormous responsibility and I was equally amazed and proud of the fact that we didn't take advantage of the situation. We still continued to perform and work. The fact is, when much is given, much is expected, and you've still got to "step up to the table." That is a great lesson, one that coaches must continue to be reminded of each year.

Y ou could see things change as we went through the time there together. Terry became protective of his privacy. There is nothing wrong with that. He became protective of his players' privacy and again there is nothing wrong with that. But it became harder the farther we went.

I always felt that Terry was torn between being only a basketball coach and his abilities to do other things—like be a lawyer, a senator, a politician, a mathematician, or a business person. He could have done any of those things. He had extraordinary intellectual abilities and to be labeled a basketball coach never seemed quite enough for him.

E ach of my mentor coaches gave me something different and something tangible that I could look back at and say, "This is what this coach did best and this is what he gave me." But the common thread among all of those coaches was their love of the game—whether it was football, basketball, or baseball—and their ability to get along with people.

Each one of them did it differently, and that was the excitement of watching them coach. In retrospect, it is very clear how each one did his job very well, but in a different way—which proves the old saying that there is no one way to do anything. There are lots of ways to do things, and great coaches always find *their* ways.


I t is important to know yourself—your strengths and your weaknesses—and then coach to your strengths and find a way to compensate for and improve your weaknesses. As a group, my mentor coaches taught me to be confident in my abilities and to be myself. One could never learn a more valuable lesson.

# Chapter 2

# Where Am I Going — and How Can I Get There?

*"The competition for jobs is as intense as the competition for good players."*

W hen you're coaching youngsters who are eight, nine, or ten years old, you are teaching fundamentals, but you are also teaching them to enjoy sports. You want them to take sports as an outlet to life, to enjoy them. Then, as you get into interscholastic sports—middle school and high school sports—it becomes more serious, but you are still teaching life's values. The skills become more precise, and the winning and losing become more defined, but the teaching really doesn't change that much.

O ne of my favorite memories about my older son, Lane, goes back to when he was about five or six years old and we were living in Durham where I was the head basketball coach at Durham High. I went to see him play tee-ball at the Durham YMCA. The teams didn't have pitchers—the kids would just hit the ball off a tee-like stand.

It was one of the first games I had ever seen him play. As a father/coach I was sitting there and I couldn't believe how nervous I was. My palms were sweaty, and every time he did something or didn't do something, I got nervous and reacted. It was a close, hard-fought game that ended up going into extra innings, only to see Lane's team lose by one run.

We got in the car and headed home. I remember that for two or three blocks I didn't know what to say to him. It was the first time I had ever seen him lose, and I didn't know how he'd react to that.

Finally, I got up enough nerve and said, "Lane, I just don't know what to say, son. You played so well and your team played so well and that was a horrible loss. I hope you are okay. Are you okay, son?" And he said, "Yeah, dad. I'm okay. It's just a game."

He was fine, but it was a very sobering moment. I was the one who wasn't all right. He was okay. At that point, he hadn't been taught that it wasn't okay to lose. It wasn't that he accepted losing, but that he had played the game for fun, the way it should be played, and that was enough.

Even today, I think Lane has his mother's balance, and they both accept reality a lot better than Ryan, my younger son, and I do.

By the time they're ten or twelve, kids begin to get the sense that winning and losing are important. Then, as they get into middle school and high school, winning becomes more urgent. Subtly, the coaches begin to emphasize winning. Winning is no longer a by-product of what you do. You begin to focus on the winning and the losing as being important.

I still say that high school coaching, public high school coaching to be specific, is the purest form of coaching there is, because it combines teaching, learning, and enjoyment — yet there is a certain measure of urgency to what you are doing. The pressure to succeed burns within the coach and the seeds of winning and losing are sown and passed on to the kids.

As you move up to the college level, there's more of a business approach to what you do. You still are coaching. You still are interacting with your athletes. You still are teaching. You still are motivating. But it's more business-like — more structure, more script, and more planning.

It seems there's more at stake. You're operating more under a microscope. The mistakes you make are seen daily — there's nowhere to hide at this level. People are going to know what you do and they are going to care about what you do because they feel you are representing them. You take them with you everywhere you go. Because there is more at stake, everything requires more forethought and planning.

I n high school, as a tenured teacher, you're obviously not going to lose your job if your team doesn't win, but there's still pressure and the pressure varies depending on where you are. In one-school towns where everybody grows up knowing where they are going to high school, there is a feeling of community pride that probably creates more pressure to win and to achieve because you are, in a sense, representing that whole town.

When kids grow up not quite sure which high school they are going to until it's time to go because the school lines often change, you don't have quite the same sense of loyalty. Town loyalties are split. A coach faces less pressure in those situations because you can say, "I'm not controlling my own destiny in terms of the players we have." You wake up one morning and somebody gives you a team and you and the players work together to make the best of the situation.

In the one-school towns you can almost pinpoint who's going to be on your team several years down the road. You can look down at the eighth grade and say, "That's my team, give or take one or two players, three years from now." Generally, there is more pressure to win in those situations.

The best thing young people can do to prepare themselves for a coaching job is to take things in proper order. No task is too menial. No team is unimportant. Learn to do the tasks as they come.

Unfortunately, that's often unrealistic because there are factors today that young people face that I never experienced—gender equity, for instance. When I went for a coaching job, women were not a factor in high school coaching. Today, it is not uncommon for women to be coaching men. Suddenly there is a large pool of candidates applying for every job. The competition for jobs is fierce.

Minorities were not a factor in coaching when I grew up. Now they are. White males once had their choice of jobs. Now, because of equal opportunity laws, being in the majority at times works to one's disadvantage. It's not practical to follow the track that I followed and have any assurance that you will "make it." Times have changed.

It's hard because there are so many obstacles along the way that you can't control. From a practical standpoint of learning the profession, there are things that I have firmly etched in my mind that my sons and their generation will never experience. They'll never really understand.

Things like sitting in a high school gym by yourself on a Saturday afternoon when everybody's gone, listening to the water drip and folding towels or uniforms after you washed them. Those things, to me, were important.

Or mopping the floor before and after every gym class and before and after every practice. Leaving the gym clean because that was my home away from home and I took pride in it.

Painting the gym. The colors hardly mattered. The building was ours and it needed a facelift. Riding on buses that broke down more often than not. Having to drive the bus on occasion. Getting my chauffeur's license! The coach was totally involved. Everything that occurred mattered, for I was responsible. No problem was too small. No job went undone. We learned by doing.

Today's young coach has mastered voice mail, e-mail, and the Internet — and thus, calls himself "coach." He (or she) is given a gas credit card, an air travel card, and a charge card. They are plastic coaches.

This generation is far less patient. I remember a conversation with my son Lane one day when he was in high school. We were in Charlottesville, Virginia, where I was an assistant at the time, and we were talking about what he wanted to do, what college he wanted to go to, and what he wanted to study when he got there.

I just threw out, "Well, what are you thinking about doing?" And he said, "Well, I want to coach." I said, "Coach?!" because I had never seen that in him. He had never shown any particular interest in coaching. He was a good athlete, but he had never talked to me about coaching at all.

So I said, "Coach? Where'd that come from?" And he said, "Looks like you're doing okay." I said, "Oh, so you want a job like mine right now? How do you see my job?"

He said, "You travel around the country and it doesn't cost you anything. You see all these great games and great players. You fly free and you eat free. You sleep free."

"When you're home, you go in early. About 11:30 you go play tennis. You get back about 1:30. During the season you have practice in the afternoons; you get through about 6:00, you come home and have a nice dinner that Mom fixes for you."

It occurred to me at that time that he really did not understand. My career started by cutting grass on the football field and dragging the baseball infield, putting the bases down and arranging for the officials. Those were special times in my life, great lessons that I could never properly explain, and he had little or no understanding of their relevance.

I honestly believe that if I was forced to go back to high school coaching it would be okay. I know times have changed, but I think I could do it. If somebody said, "You've had a successful college career, now you must finish your career in high school," I would say, "Okay."

I don't think I'd resist it because I enjoyed the close relationships, the special times, and the memories that my days as a high school coach provided. Yet to think that my sons could start in high school coaching and earn their way into the college ranks today is probably unrealistic.

Today you're fortunate to have a job, and upward mobility in the coaching profession is very difficult to achieve. You've got to do it within the system. And right now, universities and the NCAA have made it very difficult for young coaches to advance. Gender equity, cost-cutting, and general staff limitations have made the competition for jobs incredibly difficult.

Now, at the college level, every school typically has a staff consisting of the head coach, two full-time assistants, and what is referred to as a restricted duties coach. The salary for that position used to be limited to $16,000 a year. Now you can pay them whatever you want, but the job is still limited in terms of its permissible duties. The restricted duties coach is limited to on-campus recruiting only, but the position has no limitations as it relates to coaching, scouting, or team travel.

There's another animal that we've created called an administrative assistant, which is just a fancy name for a "basketball intern." People in these positions are paid as interns, basically a thousand dollars a month, and they're paid to learn the trade in an entry-level position. Securing a job as an administrative assistant is currently the best avenue and approach into college coaching.

Administrative assistants can go to practices, but they can't participate in any on-the-floor coaching. For them, permissible duties would include charting statistics, videotaping, and general note-taking. They can do administrative chores like helping with travel, writing letters, or handling recruiting lists. They can order equipment and they work at summer camps. They can observe and go to staff meetings. They are an important adjunct to the full-time staff and can learn the business from within.

Although there is no limit on how long a person can be an administrative assistant, presumably, since it's entry level, they would want to move on, and that's the way it should happen. Because they've given their time and energy to me for a couple of years, I would try to help them get a restricted duties position, or a full-time job if they are fortunate.

The dilemma comes when someone has to decide whether to accept a restricted duties job at the ACC level (or in some similar conference) or go full-time at a lower-level school. Though both are good, the jobs are different and can lead coaches in different directions. A full-time position at the lower level offers valuable recruiting experience, but limited access to upper-level coaches; a restricted duties position offers valuable access, but no recruiting experience. Thus the dilemma.

I think it's hard to go from one level to the next. And while there's nothing wrong with coaching at any particular level, if your aspirations are to be at the very highest level, you'd best stay in touch with those coaching on that level because sometimes positions are obtained just because you are there at the time. Someone could resign suddenly, and you get the job because you are available immediately. Essentially, the best coach may not get the job.

I would say that it's better to take a restricted duties job in the higher track and have the ability to interact with those people every day. It's better to be there, exchanging ideas, listening, and being seen every day, even though you won't get the practical experience of recruiting. All things being even, coaches will hire those they know and those with whom they are most comfortable.

Some people may not get jobs because a coach will say, "Well, you've never recruited, you've just been a restricted duties coach." I tend to believe that focus on recruiting is overrated. If you are talented, others will know it and you will get the chance.

B oth my sons have gone into coaching. One's a full-time assistant at East Carolina University and the other is a restricted duties coach at Furman University. My sons are sick over the game and that makes their mother ill. There's a difference between sickness and illness. The boys are sick. They are consumed with it. They are consumed almost 24 hours a day, which is unhealthy. Their mother is ill because she was hoping that they would choose lives with more stability.

L ynn has always seen a different life for them. To see both of them go into coaching was probably not something she had envisioned for her two sons. She was hoping they would choose lives with more stability. She wanted a more normal life—daughters-in-law, some grandchildren (preferably female), weekend cookouts, families coming together at normal hours—and that hasn't happened. Still, she has adjusted, as she always does, in a gracious way and has made the very most of it.

Although I was surprised when my older son announced that he wanted to go into coaching, I was maybe even more surprised when my younger son made the decision because he went to school to be a businessman. He always saw himself with a big car, nice home, and stylish clothes—and young coaches usually have to wait for those things. My older son always led a simpler life and was, in general, less demanding. While one was happy with a Volkswagon, the other yearned for a Jeep Cherokee. They are both great kids and I love them. It's just that they looked at things differently. But now they've found a common denominator in coaching. They both really love it.

I would have supported their career decisions regardless of my own feelings, because I remember my father. Even though they're doing what I'm doing, I wouldn't have discouraged them from doing something else, because I so greatly appreciated my father supporting me. Both boys went right into college coaching after graduating. Lane went to the University of Alabama as the restricted duties coach and then to East Carolina as a full-time assistant. Ryan went to the University of South Florida as an administrative assistant and then to the restricted duties position at Furman. Both chose to bypass the high school experience, going directly to college coaching. I expect them both to do very well. We will see.

Watching Lane coach gives me a feeling very similar to what I experienced when the boys were playing. As a father watching, my anxiety level is higher than when I coach, both because I have less control, and because I really want his team to perform well. I haven't been to one of Ryan's games because they've always conflicted with my schedule, but hopefully I'll see one this year.

I think I'd like to have one of my sons coaching with me at some point, but it won't happen here because there is a rule against nepotism at Wake Forest. On the other hand, maybe we wouldn't get along as well as we do now if we coached together.

When I'm through coaching, I'll do what other ex-coaches do—I'll live my coaching life vicariously through my sons.

Summer basketball camps are very important because of the exposure they provide — not only for players but for coaches, too. We've got many high school coaches working our camps, and the more exposure and experience they get, the better their chances are for landing a college job, if that's what they want. They can be seen and evaluated, plus they get a sense of what it's like working in college.

When I run a camp, the impressions that members of the staff make are very important. I notice who's enthusiastic. I notice who enjoys coaching, teaching, and relating well with the players. I also notice the coaches who are leaning up against the wall, just looking at the clock. So, it's an important chance for the young coaches to shine, and for both players and coaches to show their abilities.

The national camps — Five-Star, Nike or Adidas — offer similar opportunities, but are conducted in a more public forum with a higher level of talent. I attend these camps basically to find fresh player talent, but invariably I see a young camp coach who impresses me. I always write his name down, because you never know when you will have an opening.

D epending on the time of year, I'll get three or four requests a week inquiring about jobs. Sometimes, when the job market hits its peak in March-April-May, I may get a dozen a week. People say, "I know you don't have an opening, but I want you to put my resumé on file in case you do." The competition for jobs is as intense as the competition for good players.

As coaches, we joke about the assistant coaches' hotline. The first hour each morning seems to be devoted to job openings or the job rumor mill. The domino effect is discussed. For instance, if this guy goes here it creates an opening there and who's likely to get his job? Everybody's positioning. They're getting ready. They're making phone calls ahead, just in case. I think almost every coach wants to be a head coach at some point. The idea is to be prepared and ready when the opening occurs.

In the same way that administrative assistants have to decide about taking a restricted duties job in a less visible league, a full-time assistant has a decision to make about whether he wants to be a head coach in a less visible league or stay at a higher-level school as an assistant, in hopes that he will be around when his head coach leaves and that he's done well enough to be considered for the job.

T he job situation is discouraging for kids coming up who want to go into coaching. There are far more people who want to coach than there are jobs for them. Applying for every job that opens is not smart. It's important to know what jobs you can realistically be involved in. Last summer I talked to a young coach from the deep south about the possibility of his applying for and getting an administrative assistant job on a new, high-profile staff in the midwest. "Do you think I should apply?" he asked. "No, I don't, because you can't get it." "Why?"

"Because the coach already has his own people. Besides, you are a southerner and you presently have no midwestern contacts. I don't want you building your hopes up." Saying that was hard for me, because my friend is a fine young coach, but being realistic is necessary and shows great wisdom.

B eyond college coaching lies the fast-paced world of professional basketball. One of the things that I think would appeal to me about professional coaching is the number of games that they play. Since what I love most about coaching is the games and the game preparation—whether it's practice or planning—I would tend to believe that with more games, I would enjoy coaching more. I don't know that that's true. I think you can have too much of anything. However, I think the games and the competition and the different approaches to playing basketball at the NBA level would interest me. Certainly, coaching the best players in the world appeals to me.

I also suspect there's much more teaching at the professional level than people know. You have the tendency to think, "Well, you've got the best athletes in the world, just put them in place and let them do their thing." But I suspect there's more teaching in that league than anyone realizes, and that would also appeal to me.

I've always felt that the best coaches had the power to "hire them, play them, and fire them." Coaching a player whose situation you do not completely control is difficult. As college coaches we recruit the players, we teach them, and we decide when they play. We renew their scholarships yearly, or we help them move on. Hopefully, everything goes well all the way through to their graduation.

In the pros, most coaches don't have that level of control. However, things could be swinging back that way. Years ago, Red Auerbach and others were able to hire them, play them, and fire them, but then the NBA became very specialized. Today, the same man does not control everything. Team owners, team presidents, general managers, and coaches all have a say. Sadly, the coach is the one most affected.

But now you've got Rick Pitino going back to the Celtics and he's all-powerful. Pat Riley, John Calipari and Larry Brown have the same authority, so I think things may be changing. The players have to be answerable to the coach, otherwise you end up with the coach working for the players, and that's not good. I don't know that I would like it unless I had complete control.

A lthough you find American players going overseas to play in great numbers, you don't find American coaches working overseas very often. You do find head coaches who, for whatever reason, are out of a job, so they go coach a foreign team on a one-year basis, almost like a sabbatical. That can be financially rewarding and it can be educationally stimulating because you experience different cultures and different people. It can be fun for the family for a year; it can be a good life. However, most coaches enter such an arrangement with caution and generally on a one-year-at-a-time basis.

B eyond coaching, I think there are a number of jobs that might appeal to ex-coaches. I think in a sense all coaches are salespeople, so they generally do pretty well in the business world. Jobs that are confining are difficult for coaches. The eight-to-five kind of job with a half an hour for lunch makes us nervous. We have to have more room to maneuver, more flexibility than that. But in terms of motivating, in terms of selling, in terms of workload, I don't believe business people have anything at all on coaches. Coaches can sell and motivate; therefore, the business world would not frighten most of us.

Being a television analyst might be fun because it keeps you in touch with the game itself. There are a lot of people who have had a chance to make money out of it and still stay close to the game without the day-to-day pressure of having to win. I think there are some demands there, too, however. There's more to that job than people realize. A lot of study and planning goes into it; it doesn't just happen. Great coaches are not necessarily great analysts.

It's not wrong to coach for a long period of time, then have your batteries run dry and need a change. You may not know exactly what you want to do, but you are in a position to make the choice to step aside and let things take a natural course.

Chuck Daly did that. He coached for many years with the Detroit Pistons and did a great job with them and won two NBA championships. Then he decided to go to the New Jersey Nets, where he coached for two or three years and, no doubt, found that experience was not as satisfying as he had thought it would be.

So he backed away from coaching, did some television color work, and went into some other business ventures. But, once a coach always a coach if you really love it.

Even at sixty-six years of age or whatever he is, the passion and desire are still there, and after a couple years away from it, he felt healthy and energized and wanted to continue to coach. So, when the opportunity with Orlando came along recently, he was ready for it.

W ho's to say that someone like Dean Smith wouldn't come back—not at North Carolina, but at some other place—and coach at some point in time. It's like the old saying that you never know what you've got until you lose it. "Out of sight, out of mind" is not always true.

I n general, the coaches who take their time to learn the profession, to build a foundation of teaching and people skills, and to acquire a solid network of friends and mentors along the way, usually end up enjoying their time in the profession the most.

# Chapter 3

# Why Coaching?

*"The only reason to go into coaching is if you can't live without it."*—Paul "Bear" Bryant

Coaching is a collection of moments and experiences. It's a collage of memories that makes this thing we call coaching come alive. It's private meetings with players. It's long, late-night recruiting trips by yourself, holidays on the road, and Sunday nights on the road when everybody else is home. It's folding towels on your own. It's changing light bulbs and mopping the playing floor before practices. It's driving the bus and taking your players home after games. Those are the things that you remember the most. It's not the championships. It's not the highs and it's not a certain shot— a made shot or a missed shot or a blocked shot. That's not what makes it happen for me.

Coaching suits me. I've had the chance to mold my life in a way in which I'm comfortable. I have a structured life, but I don't like to feel like I'm in a straitjacket every day. I like the ability to be flexible.

The lifestyle is good for me. I travel easily. Flying across time zones doesn't bother me. I can go to Europe for a weekend and be back on Sunday night and not be exhausted.

39

I 'm not intimidated by people who speak different languages or live different lifestyles, or who look different than I do. I truly believe that there's good in all people and that every place has something uniquely wonderful about it. Being able to experience some of that uniqueness is one of the things that makes coaching so special. Right now there are only two states in this country that I've never been to — Montana and North Dakota. I visited South Dakota this year and Wyoming two years ago — those were the last four.

My ability to be comfortable in different situations or in unfamiliar surroundings is probably something that has improved over the years, but I never felt uneasy in strange situations. I find it hard to believe that there's any profession that exposes you to life more than coaching at the college level. You have a chance to meet so many people — all kinds of people — and it's given me an appreciation for people everywhere.

T here's a saying in sport that "you can use the ball but never let the ball use you." I think I've used the ball. It's taken me virtually all over the world. Australia is still sitting out there someplace. I'll get there in the next couple of years.

That's one reason why I wanted to go from high school coaching to college coaching. I couldn't see myself sitting in one location the rest of my life wondering what it was like in Missoula, Montana. I wanted to see it.

T he fraternity of coaching is incredible. There is a very, very strong fraternity of coaches. I don't think there is any other profession where, on any given day, two people can be bitter enemies for two hours and then when those two hours are up, put it behind them and put their arms around each other. You walk out of the arena and it's over and you move on. It's a phenomenon unlike any other.

B ear Bryant has been quoted as saying, "The only reason to go into coaching is if you can't live without it." I don't know if it's the only reason, but it's a darn good reason. I think there are those of us who, if we could—and realistically we cannot—would coach for nothing. You can't realistically do that because financially you've got to support your family. If we lived in a society where we didn't need money, then the coaching profession would be oversaturated.

T he National Association of Basketball Coaches has as its slogan, "Guardians of the Game." I think that's really good. It's really apropos, because that's what coaches are. They're guardians of the game that has been developed over the course of time. History has given us this game that we know as basketball to play and to care for. Our job is to help it get better. In a real sense, we are truly guardians.

W e need to understand the coaching profession for what it is. We're not in a life-threatening situation, so we shouldn't give it more credence than it should have. Coaches are teachers, and we need to focus on teaching and guiding young people. Coaching (and sports) provide a medium, an avenue for doing just that. We are educators, and teaching and motivating are what the coaching profession is all about.

We have been given the responsibility — the opportunity, if you will—to help guide and teach and mold young people. And there is no better way to do that than coaching kids in something that they enjoy, like basketball. When you put

kids in an environment that they enjoy, they have a tendency
to learn and it gives you a chance to impact their lives in a
positive and constructive way.

A passion for the game and a passion for the people are
the two most important traits for a coach — not necessarily in that order. I think those two things are all encom-
passing. The passion is the basis of good teaching, because if
you have a passion you want to share it. Passion indicates
that you want to share with somebody, whether it is love or
talent. So a coach with passion has a head start.

If you have passion, you motivate more easily. You have
the ability to motivate by chance, if no other way. Passion cannot be contained; it just overflows and it either has a
tendency to grab people or it turns them off. There is no middle ground for passionate people. Too much passion scares
some people.

It's possible to be a good player or a good coach and not
have an overabundance of passion. But to be truly great, a
person needs a fire that explodes. A coach needs to direct his
or her players' enthusiasm. Young players can have passion
that on occasion leads them in the wrong direction.

Freshmen, for instance, coming into a collegiate program, have a tendency to be passionate about scoring.
Because that's how they measure their success, they tend to
become distraught when they look at the post-game statistics sheet and see minimal results by their name in the scoring column.

As a coach, I have to teach them that their passion needs to be directed for the team's success first, and their individual achievements second. They also must become passionate about developing their all-around games—good defensive play, steals, and assists—as well as scoring.

B eyond a passion for people and a passion for the game, the most important requirement for good coaching is a working knowledge of your sport. You have to have a foundation, a working knowledge of the fundamentals of the game, and the ability to teach and motivate. Beyond that, you have to have a hunger for growth that's almost unquenchable. The hunger needs to be one that you can never satisfy.

Patience is key, and you've got to have great energy and resiliency. You need a sense of balance because coaching is a profession that has numerous highs and lows.

You need an understanding of the psychology of people and how to deal with their needs. You must appreciate change, because no two teams are alike, and you've got to be able to deal with change. The ability to motivate, share, and give are crucial.

W ould-be coaches or beginning coaches need to be sure they're going into coaching for the right reasons. If you are going into it primarily to win championships, you are likely to be dissatisfied. You are going to have far fewer championship years than you are going to have other years—years when you don't win the championship.

You should go into it because you enjoy working with people. Coaching is a people-oriented business and if you're not comfortable with people, or you don't enjoy interacting with them, you're probably looking at the wrong profession.

B eyond that, I think developing a strong work ethic and having fortitude are important. You need the ability to appreciate things as they occur. Young coaches need to develop understanding: in other words, to have patience. Try not to rush. Enjoy each day, each moment.

Y ou really have to have that fire in your stomach to make it, though. There's no place like being on the bench on a Saturday or Sunday afternoon and feeling the excitement and hearing the cheers of the crowd. There's just no place like that.

If you have that fire in your stomach, you have a great chance to be happy in coaching. If there is no place you'd rather be on a Saturday night than in a packed arena directing your team, you've got a chance to be a good coach.

# Chapter 4

# It's Not Always Comfortable

*"Fast is not fast enough, hard is not hard enough,
and more is always better."*

A s an assistant coach, I watched the pressure that fans and media put on two head coaches—Carl Tacy at Wake Forest and Terry Holland at Virginia.

I've seen the effects of negative articles in the papers— articles that were critical of their coaching decisions or their recruiting or just "Why did they do that?" types of articles.

I think sometimes the media lashes you whether you need it or not, just to prove their objectivity, and maybe that's okay. Some time ago, an article appeared and when Dan Collins, a well-respected area sportswriter, came in my office I said, "Well, I took my once-a-year obligatory lashing yesterday, didn't I." He just laughed and said "Oh, I didn't hit you that hard."

S omewhere about the middle of my Virginia years I realized that you can't fight these guys because they've got the pens in their hands and they're always going to have the last word.

I also decided, "Why should I worry about it when they don't really know what happened? They weren't at practice. They don't know why a particular decision was made. They don't know why Player A played as opposed to Player B because they didn't see the fact that Player B loafed in practice every day, or perhaps failed to execute. They are reporting what they observe and what they believe to be true. They are being paid to report and create interest."

There's a new phenomenon we call recruiting tabloids, which document recruiting from beginning to end. Self-proclaimed experts insist that their "inside information" is more accurate than someone else's or that this recruiting class is stronger than that one. It is absolutely mind-boggling that the public follows recruiting so closely.

I watched Terry Holland as he struggled with negative and critical articles. There were two or three writers in Virginia who, every time they wrote something, caused him discomfort. So I finally suggested, "Okay, let's not read the paper, particularly during the season."

I don't think I ever got him to quit reading the paper, but I stopped, and gradually I began to feel better. Philosophically, I see no reason to read or listen to outsiders' opinions. I continue to remind myself that they know much less than I know about my team.

Even today, I don't read anything in the paper that has to do with Wake Forest. One of my great loves in the morning is to get a cup of coffee and look at the scores. After I walk my dog, I come back in and get my cereal and my coffee, sit down, and open the paper. I have trained myself to go straight to the scores. Then I close the paper and put it up. I almost never read articles that are analytical or that report on games.

I even try not to read articles about other teams. When I come into the office, if one of my staff says, "You need to read this," then I'll look at it, but they know that basically I don't read the paper.

I f you do read articles about yourself or your team, what invariably happens is that you end up getting mad at the person who wrote it. And you have to continue to deal with them, so there's no reason to create antagonism. A big part of a head coach's job at the college level is media relations. I try to make that part as pleasant as possible. If I don't know that the beat writer wrote a negative article about us then I'm not mad at him or her the next time we talk. I'm able to focus better on my team and I'm not concerned by what he or she thinks or wrote.

T here's a difference between being a friend and being a loyal friend. I think they are two different relationships. A friend is somebody you care about and support. You are there for them.

A loyal friend, I think, is a different matter. As a loyal friend you have the right — more than that, you have the responsibility — to make decisions for your friend. I hope I have loyal friends in this office.

As a basketball coach at Wake Forest, I'm going to have things written or said about me: "He's not as good a coach as, say, Mike Krzyzewski" or "He made a poor decision there" or whatever it happens to be. There are some things that I may need to know, but I don't need to know *now*. And there are other things that I never need to know. Loyal friends—loyal colleagues—have the responsibility to make those decisions in my best interest. They can make those decisions because they understand me and they know how that knowledge might adversely affect me.

M ail from fans—positive or negative—though considerable, does not make up the biggest portion of my daily mail. The largest number of letters comes from fund-raising charity events asking me to donate items for auctions or to be used as prizes. The second biggest category is appearance requests, generally for me, but on occasion for me and a player. I get letters asking, "Could Tim Duncan please come read to my third-grade class?" The requests are so numerous that, though all seem to be worthy, at some point we must say, "No." Most of the requests are legitimate and deserve our efforts. But it's just impossible to do everything and still allow players or coaches to have lives of their own.

I t's often hard for college players to handle the constant demands of being in the public eye, of being recognized and asked for autographs, especially in their private time. It depends upon the player, but I think generally they do feel infringed upon. They feel watched and uncomfortable. If they're in a group, they feel protected, but if just one or two players go out, they try to stay out of the limelight. They try to avoid the most popular places and find their own space. I know Tim Duncan did.

When Ralph Sampson was at Virginia, Coach Holland made a rule that Ralph could not sign autographs while he was eating in public. It was a good rule, one that was used effectively. Without such a rule as a buffer, the stars might never finish their meals.

W e haven't had a "no autograph" rule here at Wake Forest, but instead of eating in public as a team we call ahead to a restaurant and get a private room. You tell your players to be as obliging as they possibly can, up to a point, yet you don't want their individual time infringed upon to the point where they can't eat.

About the only other thing that we do is make sure that the players all have unlisted telephone numbers and unlisted addresses, both on campus and off campus. That protects them and their privacy about as much as is reasonable.

You want your players to be a part of everyday campus life and you don't want to segregate them or separate them from the campus itself. We've required that all our players live on campus until at least their senior years, because I want them to be regular students as much as is humanly possible.

H owever, at the end of the first semester of his junior year, Tim Duncan came to me and said, "Coach, I know I'm not allowed to live off campus until next year. But I'm going to ask that you consider letting me do that now, even if I keep my room on campus. I have a friend who I've known since we were freshmen together who I can stay with." I asked, "Timmy why do you want to move off campus now?"

And he said, "Well, it's really hard because everybody knows where I live and people come by, sometimes in the middle of the night, asking for autographs for friends or family back home. And while I don't mind doing that, it's just that I'm not getting enough rest right now. We're getting ready to head into the important part of our season and I really feel it would be better if I separated myself from that type of thing now."

So we let him move, although he did sleep some of the time on campus. I think on game nights he was always off campus so that he could get the amount of rest he needed.

W hen our players go out in public, we want them to
be obliging, but we don't have any specific rules.
We tell them just to be courteous and always try to treat
people like they would want to be treated themselves. I
think for the most part our fans are considerate and don't
overdo it.

We explain to our players that when they go out in public
they represent Wake Forest University, our basketball team,
and their families—and that they need to act accordingly. Because they are basketball players, they do have this added responsibility. By and large, they all do very well with that.

College is a time of growth and a time for kids to try
their wings. Our players know pretty well what they can do
and I think most of them enjoy being college students.


T here's been a big push in the last three or four years to
allow the student-athlete to be as normal as he or she
can possibly be. The NCAA has mandated that you can only
take up so many hours of their week for athletic purposes.

For instance, if you are going to have preseason conditioning, you can only condition them for eight hours a week
and that's it. During the season, you can only occupy them
for 20 hours a week, which includes games. The idea is to
give them time to study, relax, and socialize, much as non-
athletes do.

Strangely enough, the NCAA doesn't count public ser-
vice-related time. The rule concerns only basketball-related
activities. Apparently the NCAA looks at public service as
being good for the players—an important part of their personal development and their responsibility as public role
models.

Our players do things like that—going to visit hospitals, ministering to kids that are deprived in some way, and
attending leadership conferences. I think we have an obliga-

tion to help others. We want to encourage that. But it does create terrific demands on their time and a careful balance must be found.


I n general, coaches understand that they will be criticized. The very nature of the job puts you out there and opens you up to criticism. So that doesn't really bother us. But when the criticism becomes personal and hurtful, then even the most hardened veteran becomes annoyed and bothered by it. If you acknowledge it, constant criticism can cause you to become reclusive.

I've seen it happen over and over again to coaches. Coaches who are by nature outgoing, gregarious, happy people become withdrawn because of severe criticism and a fear of public confrontation. After games — win or lose — instead of relaxing and enjoying their family or friends or staff, they choose to go home, close the door, and work some more. They put on the tape and look at the game again, or rehash it with their staff behind closed doors.

They let that behavior extend to the off nights, as well. When others are having cookouts with friends in the neighborhood, they stay at home. They choose not to go to movies or take their wives out to dinner. They just circle the wagons, a strategy designed to keep the world outside. And they only confide in those they know they can trust and those who are going to watch their backs all the time.


S ome people are friendly to you because of what you do, not necessarily because of who you are. At times, you might not trust their motives for offering their friendship. You don't know if they like you for *who* you are or if they like you for *what* you are. And if they like you for *what* you are, that could mean they want something from you.

So you hold them at arm's length until you find out, and then you make a decision. That's the way coaches subconsciously react.

W hen you go out to dinner, you learn to live with the whispers and the requests for autographs, and you just smile and go on. I'm amused by it sometimes, and I've learned to avoid it by dressing down. I'm most recognizable when I wear my glasses because that's the way people see me on TV—that's the way I am at games. If I don't wear my glasses to the grocery store, people don't recognize me quite as readily. So if I put a baseball cap on and don't wear glasses, I can go pretty much anywhere inconspicuously.

M y sons grew up at half-court of the ACC tournaments, so they knew the good, the bad, and the ugly. They knew what to expect. They knew it wasn't going to be a chariot ride the whole time. Sometimes people are going to lash you even when you don't deserve it.

It's interesting to see how my family handles the criticism. My wife handles it with grace and dignity; she's the consummate coach's wife. She can smile when people are hurtful and smile when people are kind. You wouldn't know the difference. That doesn't mean that she doesn't have feelings, but she's not given to shows of emotion. She rarely has heavy swings of emotion.

One of my sons is somewhat like her. The other one, however, is more volatile. He's more given to mood swings and he does react to his environment. He's likely to chest up against a spectator who's calling his dad names, and there are reports that he has done just that in the stands.

P ressure manifests itself in different ways. It can also come from different sources: fans, media, the university —or it can be self-imposed. Regardless, it's very difficult to live and work and do your best if you are afraid. In fact, I think it's almost impossible to do so.

I can't allow myself or my team or others around me to be concerned about how long we're going to be in this particular place—that is, as a head coach at Wake Forest, an assistant coach at Wake Forest, or a player at Wake Forest. You really can't be productive or enjoy yourself if you are worried about when you might lose your job. It is difficult enough to do well under normal circumstances. Allowing standards set by others to complicate your job is distracting and unfair.

W hen I'm put in a decision-making position, I usually look at the two extremes. I ask myself, "What's the best thing that can happen and what's the worst thing that can happen?" If I can determine the answer to both questions, my decision is usually made for me. Usually I can figure it out. When you look at winning and losing in basketball—at whatever level—the best far outweighs the worst.

I'm not going to starve. If I lose my job, I'm going to continue to eat. Things tend to get out of proportion. Young coaches don't understand it because they've never been through it. They're pushing to get ahead as quickly as possible. Fast is not fast enough, hard is not hard enough, and more is always better. Ironically, these coaches are the ones most affected by pressure.

T he competition to get ahead is more pronounced every year. We all fall into the trap of trying to get ahead as quickly as we possibly can, rather than taking our time with it. We don't see the game or the profession for what it really is. It should be something fun and something that we enjoy, but because we push so hard, we end up not enjoying what we do. I think it drives a lot of really good coaches out of the profession.

Coaches who are totally consumed by the winning and the losing are likely to fall prey to burnout faster than those who concentrate on the processes that enable you to win. Those who make it to the mountaintop in sports have perspective and understand that winning and losing are only products of the collective efforts that we make. The knowledge that we gave our all lasts forever. Those who only concentrate on the end result of winning a game are candidates for burnout far more than people who coach for the sheer love of the game and the experience of coaching.

I n anything that involves competition you have a tendency to fall prey to burnout, but the difference in coaching at this level, versus being an accountant who crunches numbers or a financial planner who's responsible for money, is that the mistakes that you make in coaching are magnified because they are so public. As coaches you are saddled by the burden of public opinion. Some might say that we are tried daily in the court of public opinion.

If you handle your best friend's money and you lose $100,000 one day, you may get it back the next day if the market turns. Even if it doesn't turn, the results will usually not be found in the paper the next day.

Whereas if you have a series of losses, or your team fails to play up to expectations, or things just don't go your way, you are held accountable in the court of public opinion. This pressure causes you to get into a vacuum of "achieve now, succeed now, win now" — or else.

Y ou only have so much physical and emotional energy, and if you expend it all as a youth or as a young coach, then there's nothing left in the later years. So, the early pace of coaching and the pressure to move quickly within the profession encourages burnout.

Other professions where burnout is prevalent would be in fields dealing with life or death—surgeons, for instance, are constantly faced with life-and-death decisions. Air traffic controllers who have planes full of people that they must safely guide through a series of takeoffs and landings are certainly vulnerable to pressure. Anyone who works under continual time pressure is also subject to burnout. But because coaches operate in such a public venue, we may be more vulnerable than most.

W inning and losing are the same, regardless of the level. I remember moving from Durham High School to college coaching as an assistant here at Wake Forest. We played in the Big Four Tournament which used to be held at the beginning of the season and involved North Carolina, North Carolina State, Duke, and Wake Forest. It was my first college experience and, as luck would have it, we won the tournament. I remember going toward the locker room after the game and a writer from Durham, Keith Drum, somehow got shoulder-to-shoulder with me and asked if I felt more pressure in that venue, with 17,000 people watching, than I had in our championship years at Durham High School.

It dawned on me that there was no difference, because what you put into a situation determines the amount of pressure you feel or the emotion that you have for that event. And once you've given your all, then there is no more you can give. The pressure can be no greater. It is always the same.

A nother area of pressure for coaches is that of legal liability. It would be unbearable to go to work every day
and feel as if you were walking on eggshells or that anything
you did could be used against you. You'd lose the level of
comfort that you need. Maybe we don't need to be too comfortable, but at the same time, we don't need to be too para-
noid, either.

S omehow you need to feel like you are doing what's right
without having everybody—the arm of the law included
—looking over your shoulder all the time. We worry about
today's hot topics such as harassment, taking away an individual's rights, or making sure an individual has due process.
Coaches, particularly the older coaches, are unaware of the
pitfalls of the liability of sport. We are without formal training. The younger coaches are getting more and more training
as they go through college now, but the older coaches still
work somewhat exposed. It's not very comfortable.

You're actually much more protected against physical
risk and liability. At this level, we have such good medical
care that doctors really are the ones that make the decisions,
not coaches. In other words, if a doctor evaluates an athlete
and says he or she is capable of playing, you're going to be
okay. If the doctor said a player was unable to play, and you
played him anyway, then you would become legally liable.
But at this level, that's not going to happen. I don't know of a
coach who would play a kid if the doctor hadn't given per-
mission.

I think you've got a bigger problem at the high school
level simply because medical expertise is not as available.
The kids have their annual sports physicals and, if you're
lucky, you've got family doctors to help look after you. In
areas where there are top hospitals like Duke Medical Center
in Durham, Memorial Hospital in Chapel Hill, or N.C. Bap-
tist Hospital in Winston-Salem, you're in pretty good shape.

But when you're in rural areas where you don't have special-ists in sports medicine, it becomes a bit more risky. Coaches would be wise to take more care and be more prudent in their decision making as to whether a kid should play or not.

W hen all is said and done, we're still talking about a game here. We're not talking about curing a life-threatening disease or a high-level crime. We're talking about a game and the development of the game, and the develop-ment of a group of people. In the end, the most important thing that we're doing is trying to grow as people.

I 've chosen to concentrate on the things that I can control, not the things that I cannot control. Worrying about what *might be* is a burden in itself— and it's worry that you do not need.

# Chapter 5

# Seasons of Coaching

*"Once you've been in the arena, I don't know
how you can ever be satisfied with anything else."*

T he natural passion that I have for competition has been
the one constant in my career. I don't feel that's dimin-
ished at all. If anything, it's intensified as I've gotten older.

I really do enjoy coaching, and at times I think how amazing it is that I can do what I do and get paid for it. If you
could actually coach for nothing, that would be the best.
Outside of being a great coach, one reason that Dean Smith
has been at his best after so many years of being a head
coach in the ACC is because financially he didn't have to
coach any more. He could walk away anytime — as he did —
and people couldn't put pressure on him. The only pressure
he felt was the pressure he wanted to feel. That's when it's
the best. But when the pressure that one does feel puts things
out of balance, as it inevitably does with all of us, then it's
good to recognize that and step back from it.

Some of the best high school coaches are probably those
who are in their second careers. For instance, someone who
coached 30 years in the public schools and then coaches at a
private school not only has his state retirement, but also has

the private school salary that he doesn't really depend upon to live.

Those men usually are financially secure. Coaching is great if you don't have financial pressures to worry about. You will rarely hear second-career coaches lament, "If I lose my job, I'm out and then my family won't eat and what will we do?" They coach for the love of it.

S ometimes in coaching, as in life, you tolerate certain things so that you can do others. I happen to be one who likes recruiting, but some people tolerate recruiting so that they can coach. The part of my job that I find distasteful is the paperwork. I don't like the memos and the voice mail and the letter writing and that kind of thing, although I think I'm pretty good at it and I keep up with it.

But I do that so I can coach, and so I can recruit. And I coach so that I can get to the scene of the battle. The thing that makes everything else worthwhile is the two-hour block of time in which we test ourselves against our opponents in the games. It's totally exhilarating.

P ersonally, I enjoy the practices almost as much as I enjoy the games. But it remains that if we didn't have the games, we could never really know how to measure our progress. We must always test ourselves in two ways: practices and games.

You can only test yourself so much. That's what you do in practice, you test yourself. Some people say that you are actually playing against yourself in games. I think that's true up to a point, but you can't control some of the things that happen in a game. For instance, I have no control over the defense that my opponent plays, or which players they choose to play, or when they are on the court.

A fter I had been in college work for two or three years, I remember my mother asking me what I did in the off-season. It was her belief that since basketball season lasted only five or six months, there were another six months or so to fill. I remember just quietly grinning and thinking, "If people only knew!"

You are at least as busy out of the season as you are in the season. The difference is that what you are doing changes, and there is a lessening of the everyday pressure to win.

In the off-season you don't feel that constant pressure to achieve and to get better each and every day. You want to get better as a program, better as a coach, better as a staff, and better as a university, but you don't feel the urgency to do it *that day*.

C oaching really is a seasonal occupation. July, which is the beginning of most fiscal years, is filled with recruiting. From the recruiting standpoint, it's what we call an evaluation period. It's the time when Division I coaches hit the road. We go to every nook and cranny, every city, every small town, and in some cases, every country, that we can get to in about a three-week period.

We can talk to potential recruits on the phone, but we can't visit with them. We can't go to their homes. We can go to their towns and watch them play on the playground or in summer leagues or in their gyms, but we can't sit down and have a conversation with them.

The bulk of the recruiting money that's spent is spent in July. As a staff, we try to plan carefully so that we're not criss-crossing with each other. Some staffs split up the travel geographically, but we just go wherever the prospects are. We try to be economical, but it's a no-holds-barred period. It's an all-out attack on seeing as many players as you can see who might meet the needs of your program in the next few years.

It is an ordeal that takes its toll on each coach, but the time to recruit is limited, so you go, and you are relentless. The period goes on for about 21 days, usually beginning right after July 4. At the end of July, you sit down with your staff and you share with each other who you saw, who you liked, and which prospects you would like to actively recruit.

Mixed in, you are probably going to have a camp of your own and maybe a couple of speaking engagements. Summer school is going on and you try to keep up with your players who may be around. There is very little personal time during this time.

July is a time when you send your wife and kids to the beach and tell them you'll see them in three or four weeks. That's the kind of life you lead then. The recruiting process that begins in July consumes much of your time and energy off and on for the next several months. It is tiring and demanding, yet it is crucial to the success of any program. Recruiting starts in July and comes together later.

August is the month in which you finish up summer school and clean things up from the summer. It's one of the few times when you can kick back a little, and it's the time when most basketball coaches take some private or family time. If there is any down time in a coach's life, it's in August because it's the lead-in to the new year and you want to be fresh and rested when your players report to school.

Occasionally, this period may be interrupted by a foreign tour with your team or conducting foreign clinics. I've had people ask me to come to Europe to speak, but typically I won't go unless I take my family with me because it's a time we want to be together.

School starts so early now that students are coming in by the third week of August, so the month is short and your vacation ends all too soon.

S eptember is spent getting your freshmen adjusted, mesh-
ing your returnees with your freshmen, setting up lines of
leadership, and getting everybody settled in their classes. Our
team also begins preseason conditioning work. Our support
staff members — weight coaches and conditioning coaches —
are in charge of that, but I like to stay in touch with the
process each day.

I try to go to as many football games as I can because I
enjoy them. But weekends are the times I do a lot of my
speaking at coaching clinics, and I'm on the road a lot during
this period, so it's hard for me to be present for each one. If
we have six home games and I see three of them, I feel lucky.

There's another round of recruiting in September, though
this time period is different. There's a three- or four-week
window of time during which you can talk to the prospects.
It's in September that we begin to build on the work that we
did in July. In August my staff sets up September appoint-
ments for me to go in and meet with families, meet with the
kids, and meet with the high school coaches or anybody else
that we feel is involved in the recruiting process.

As the head coach, I do most of the initial face-to-face
contacts with the recruits and their families. I think it's important that the head coach be the main contact. My assistants
have to do a lot of the background work and usually pave the
way for my meetings. But when it comes time to sit down and
talk, I must handle that because the players and their families
have to understand me and I have to understand them.

The September time period is difficult to schedule. There
is so much to do and so many places to go that careful planning is required. Our team needs my attention, yet the recruiting process is important as well. It's often hard to balance.

W hen we get back around October 10, I generally have
two or three days set aside for our staff to get to-

gether without interruption and we map out plans for the beginning of practice on the Saturday closest to October 15. Once practice begins, the team's progress becomes my main focus. Recruiting becomes secondary. Most of the work is done; we just wait it out. I might make an occasional recruiting call or write an occasional letter, but I turn my attention to my team—every day, all day. It's hard to balance that with the recruiting, the academics, and the speaking. It's hard to put all that together, but the team's development is the most important.

I try to keep up with what's going on across the university because I am very interested, but it's hard. I don't want people to think I'm being rude, because I am proud of the achievements of the university, but timewise, it's hard. After we start practice, for a period of one month that's all I do— practice and take care of the academics. I monitor the recruiting, but we don't travel anymore.

I n November, we start our games. I do some speaking at clinics and other events, and a few personal appearances, but those are one-day obligations at most. Nobody would choose to be a banquet speaker. Actually, I guess there *are* people who make their living giving talks, but that's not why coaches do it. The practices and the games are what it's all about and everything is scheduled around those times.

Before you know it, Thanksgiving arrives, followed by Christmas, and suddenly it's conference time. You play into the first week or so of March and then comes the ACC Tournament and, hopefully, post-season play. That's literally the way the season goes, and our basketball team consumes virtually all of my time. I try to get one day for Christmas and feel fortunate if I get that much. The players will probably go home around the 23rd and come back the 26th. If our team has a trip somewhere at Christmastime, then they wouldn't get to go home at all.

The season is a blur. Staff meetings, film and scouting reports, player workouts, and team practices are non-stop. We do not work on Sunday mornings, but we come in early Sunday afternoons and are in the office until 9:00 p.m. or later. The team will practice six days a week. The NCAA mandates that we give them one day off. Practice and team activities cannot exceed twenty hours a week.

O nce you experience the competition and what it's like to sit on a bench and coach, it's hard to get that out of you. No matter how your team did during the season, there is always a letdown when it's over, a period of withdrawal. It's very hard.

It's probably worse for a high school coach than it is for a college coach because we start recruiting immediately once the season ends. We turn our attention quickly to what we can do to improve. For a high school coach, only the next year is left. I always found the season's end much harder for me as a high school coach than it has been as a college coach.

I t's in the months of April and May that I do all of my speaking to alumni groups. I usually do twelve to fifteen meetings, mostly in the Southeast. The events usually focus on the past season, a quick glance ahead to next year, and a subtle pitch about fundraising. Giving speeches or interviews has always been easy for me. I'm not saying I'm good at it, just that it's easy for me. It's easy because I am talking about something I know about.

Coaches also have various conference meetings to go to and the national convention that meets in conjunction with the Final Four. Recruiting stops around April 15 and then we've got about three weeks of school left. We then turn our attention to our players and their academic concerns. Exams begin the last week in April and are over the first of May. The players get two weeks off and then come back for summer school.

J une is a month filled with basketball camps. At Wake Forest, we have several of our own camps during the month. Just about every school has a camp of some description. Running a basketball camp is a tremendous responsibility, but is usually worth the effort. It's good for the university and for the coach.

I tell the kids that come to my camp that there are only two reasons to come. The first is because you want to solidify the base of basketball skills that you have and take your game to another level if you can. Realistically, in one week of basketball camp you're not going to go from who you are to being Michael Jordan. It's just not going to happen. But you can be better at the end of one week, and that's one of our objectives.

The second reason to go to a camp is of a social nature. Kids need exposure to people from other geographic areas, other ways of life, other religions, other ethnic groups, and other races, and they can get that at camp. They learn to live and play with people different from themselves. For instance, I received a letter from a kid from North Carolina asking for the address of a kid from Miami whom he met at camp. He wanted to write and see if his new friend from Miami would room with him next year. I enjoy watching youngsters come together as friends as much as I enjoy watching their basketball skills improve.

I usually have some speaking engagements and appearances at charity events in June and then we're back to July 1 and it starts all over again.

F or a high school coach, the summer months are usually spent scurrying around trying to find summer work.

Some of them work in the summer camps of colle[
coaches and some of them have their own camps. A lot of
them teach driver's education. Some of them work for the
local recreation department. There are various ways that
high school coaches can make money in the summertime.
The lucky ones are on eleven- or twelve-month contracts
instead of the normal ten-month contracts held by most
teachers.

A high school coach's year starts around August 1 because most of them coach football. They'll spend August
through November in football. Depending on the situation,
a coach may have a couple of weeks overlap with basketball
or another fall sport. It varies with the coach, but typically
coaches coach every season. They want to, not only because
it means more money for them, but because they love
coaching.

Throughout the various athletic seasons, coaches also
teach their academic classes, but they don't have other outside responsibilities to the extent that a college coach might.
The work they do centers around their teams and their teaching assignments in the school and then, to a lesser degree,
whatever other responsibilities they may have from a community standpoint.

Most of the time, high school coaches coach at least two
and sometimes three seasons. Someone may be a head coach
in one sport and an assistant coach in another sport, but
they're usually involved in multiple sports and multiple seasons. If their coaching seasons overlap, then they have to
schedule their practices carefully—one team in the afternoon
and the other in the evening. That's what I did as a high
school coach. Their holidays depend on where and when
they coach, but they will have more time off than a college
coach. A high school basketball coach could get as much as a
week off from basketball at Christmastime if he schedules
carefully.

H igh school coaches always have to remember that they
are hired as educators first and that they're hired to
teach—that athletics are looked upon as being extracurricu-
lar. In college, we work full-time as coaches. It's not extracur-
ricular. But as a high school educator, you're hired to teach
first, yet you are expected to work diligently with your athletes, though never at the expense of your teaching. That's
the way it should be. Coaches *should* think of themselves as
teachers. They teach subjects, but they also teach the game.

W hen you look back at the different seasons and teams
that you've coached, each one of them has its own
special moments and memories. Some years you feel more
inept or inadequate than others. Some years almost everything seems to go right. Coaches know their teams so well
that we tend to know what kind of season we're likely to be
facing. I think the time in the off-season gives you time to
mentally adjust—to the good and bad.

I 've had very few seasons in which I was completely surprised. Generally, I might know that we're going to be better next year, or I might suspect that we will struggle to be as
good. I don't usually get fooled by much. Every once in a
while, though, you're surprised by what happens in a season.
My '96–'97 team surprised me because we didn't play our
best basketball at the end of the year.

A s I think back over the eight years that we've had here
at Wake Forest, I can't think of one that has really
thrown me for a loop. The only real disappointments that I
have had are the years in which I didn't connect with my
team—really didn't connect all year long—and I think there
were only two of those years. One of them was this past year,

'96–'97. I don't think we really connected. Getting along and connecting as one are two different things. I never felt that I had a real pulse on our team.

I don't know whether Tim Duncan's status as a superstar had anything to do with that or not. I don't think there was any kind of resentment towards Tim. I think it was more a feeling of: "He's here. He's going to carry us. The rest of us don't have to do as much."

I loved my team individually, but I did not *like* my team collectively. That doesn't mean that they weren't good kids, for they were. If anything, they were too nice. We just didn't have the competitive fire that we needed down the stretch—and I failed to bring it out.

There was one other team—it was actually my second team here—that I never could get together. They didn't fight, but it was a mixed team. I had some players that I recruited and some who were left over from Bob Staak's tenure. They were good kids and they were really as talented a team as I've had, but I just never got them to trust me. It was almost as if each one of them had his own agenda.

The other six years have been wonderful. It is disappointing not to connect with your team. Saying, "I didn't like my team" is a bit strong, but I didn't enjoy my relationship with my team. When you don't totally connect, it's hard to fully enjoy the experience.

A s I look back at my high school years, I think I coached almost as I played. I was involved in every simple pass, every catch, every shot, every rebound, every block out—everything. If I had continued like that for 32 years I'd probably be a nervous wreck. I couldn't have done it. But I think it was good for me at the time and it was good for my teams.

I'm certainly less emotional now. That's the area that I've worked on the most—being able to control my own emotions so that I can stay in control of my own faculties. I can think better under pressure now. Experience teaches you to handle pressure, but I'm not sure that coaches can feel the game quite the way players might. However, I probably make better decisions because I'm somewhat removed from it.

O nce you've been in the arena, once you've been down on the bench, once you've been involved in the game itself, I don't know how you can ever be satisfied with anything else. When I go to games now, unless one of my own is playing or coaching, it's hard for me to get interested. I have a hard time just watching as a spectator.

Being a participant is everything. Having an effect on the way the game turns out—unless you've done that, I don't think anybody can truly understand what it's like.

There is nothing like walking into the Joel Coliseum at night and seeing 14,407 people in the stands as the starting line-ups are announced and hearing the public address announcer reel off the names one after the other. Whether you are home or away—there is nothing like that. It's really special.

A t some point you may have enough of it, but I don't think you can ever replace it with another type of joy. You can walk away from it and say, "It's time for me to do some other things. I want to spend more time with my family. I want to vacation. I want to travel. I want to play golf. I want to play tennis. I want to write." But when all is said and done . . .

You'll never reach that high again. It's a high that you cannot attain in any other profession. You can be content to do other kinds of things because you've experienced it and you feel good about your experience. But you can't walk away from it and say that you'll reach that high in another profession, in another way. I don't know anybody who's been able to do that. I've had lots of friends who have walked away from it and say that they're just as happy now as they ever were, but when it gets right down to it, they still live their lives vicariously through those of us still coaching.

I have friends who call me weekly during the season wanting to know what went into a certain decision, or what I'm going to do about a certain player, or who I'm recruiting. They still live their lives through us. It's special.

C oaching as a career is not as attractive for players as it used to be. They see the pitfalls and they know that it's hard to coach for a long time. They see that the opportunities to coach are few and far between and that it's hard to get to this level.

Since they're part of it, the players know how hard it is to deal with today's generation. Randolph Childress once told me that he would never coach because he said he "didn't want to put up with what you guys have to put up with." I think that really is more of a prevalent attitude than any of us will admit. Players know what the demands are and they know what you have to put up with and they don't want to mess with it.

W hen all is said and done, I think I've been very fortunate to keep everything going through 32—starting 33—years.

# Chapter 6

# Relationships

*"You don't know the true measure of a man
until you sit beside him on a bench."*

## Other Coaches

There's a tremendous bond and respect from one coach to the other and that's healthy. Since we understand the demands of our own jobs, we understand the pressure that others are under as well. You're in the most dramatic of situations and then, once the competition is over, you go back to being friends. For the most part, coaches have the ability to do that. It's really not surprising that coaches get along outside of the public eye.

Sports also teach that. You shake hands before the game and you shake hands after the game. It's almost part of our mores. It's just something you do, that you are taught to do. Symbolically, it's something you do, but hopefully the handshake has a deeper meaning.

There's no question that's one reason why the idea of coaching appeals to young boys and girls. Nobody appreciates your problems like you do, except other coaches. In the best of times, coaches are there. But also, more importantly, in the worst of times, coaches are always there when other coaches need them most. They are always there. Always.

T his has never been more true than when I was a college junior and playing basketball at Guilford College for Coach Jerry Steele. Coach Steele, who had only been out of college a few years, was barely older than his players, and we were very close.

One Thursday night we were playing at North Carolina Wesleyan College in Rocky Mount. The night was memorable for two reasons—one, we played very well and won the game, but even more important, it was the last night I ever saw my dad alive. My mom and dad had driven the 44 miles from Goldsboro to Rocky Mount to see us play, and after the game they waited to see me. I showered hurriedly because I knew that the team always pulled out immediately after games and I wanted to have as much time with them as possible.

My dad had not been very healthy the last three or four years, but he had turned the corner health-wise and was doing really well at the time. We had a great chat and I remember the ride home and how good I felt about him and my mother and just how proud I was that they were both at the game.

The next afternoon we practiced in Greensboro and then left for Newberry College in Newberry, South Carolina. As was typical in those days, the visiting team stayed in a room in the gymnasium because teams back in the sixties playing at the NAIA level really didn't have a lot of money in their budgets. Each school helped out by providing overnight lodging for the visiting team. The beds were usually the double-decker, barracks-type, but it was all right. It was all we knew.

Our game was 7:30 p.m. and, as was usually the case, the team rested for a couple of hours in the afternoon. I rarely ever went to sleep because I'm not much of a sleeper during the day.

I was lying there and Coach Steele's assistant and my good friend, Roy Williams, tiptoed into the room and said, "Coach needs to see you." I said, "Now?" and he said, "Yeah."

I knew that was unusual. Coach Steele and I talked a lot since I was the point guard and he wanted us to be in concert with each other mentally, but he had never wanted to meet during rest time before.

I got up out of my bed and I walked into the room and I noticed that Roy didn't go into the room with me. That just heightened my level of anxiety. If it had been a basketball issue, Roy would have gone in and we would have had a three-way conversation.

When I walked in, Coach Steele was sitting in a chair with his head lowered, almost staring at the floor. The strangest sensation came over me. He looked up at me as I sat down and out of my mouth came the words, "My dad is dead, isn't he?"

To this day, I really can't explain how I knew it, but I knew he'd died. Coach didn't say a word. His head just went back down. It was the strangest feeling I'd ever had in my life.

My Aunt Grace, who lived in South Carolina, and her family were coming that night to see us play and I thought maybe I could play the game and then get them to take me back home so that I could be there when Mother woke up the next morning. I suggested that option to Coach Steele and told him I really wanted to play that night. I told him that I was certain that my dad would want me to play.

He said, "Let me think about it." When I called my mother she said, "Do what you feel is right." I went back in to see Coach Steele to reiterate my desire to play. Again he said, "Let me think about it."

We went to the pre-game meal and he didn't mention anything to the team and I didn't mention it to the team, though I think everybody could sense something was different. The game began and I was not in the starting line-up for the first time that season. We lost the game, but he didn't play me that whole night.

After the game, Coach Steele talked to the team about the situation. It was very emotional being in the room as he spoke. I was surprised when he closed his talk to the team by saying, "David and I are leaving now to go back to Goldsboro to be with his family." In other words, he was taking himself away from the team to be with me when he knew that I needed it most.

We drove through the night to get back to Goldsboro. I remember we drove in about five o'clock in the morning just before the dark gave way to dawn.

He stayed most of the day, and then went back to Greensboro, packed some clothes, and came back for the funeral. Times like that really bond people together.

It was probably a five- or six-hour drive from Newberry to Goldsboro and there were long stretches of time where there was no sound except the popping of knuckles. That's all there was. But there was also some really poignant conversation between the two of us that's still with me today.

Coach Steele is still coaching at High Point University in High Point, NC, and I recently was privileged to speak at a university banquet honoring his 25 years there. The banquet was attended by over 800 people.

S omething somewhat similar happened to one of our players at Wake Forest. While we were down at Florida State, we found out that Tony Rutland's mother had been diagnosed with incurable cancer. During the pre-game meal there was an emergency phone call for me from Tony's father. I took the phone call and came back and talked to the team, but didn't tell anyone about the call.

I had told Tony's father that if he wanted Tony not to play and to go home that night I'd send him, but he insisted that Tony should play and then come home the next morning. After the meal, everybody went back to their rooms and I asked Randolph Childress, our team captain, to go with me to talk to Tony. We told him that it didn't look like his mother was going to make it and that I would send him home the next day. That was the bad part.

The good part was that she did live for a little more than a year. She fought hard, and many lessons were learned during that time, but eventually she succumbed. Watching that kind of ordeal, you realize that we are really affected by death much more than by life. It causes you to come face-to-face with your own mortality.

C oaches try to cause each other to lose their jobs and then we try to help them keep them. I don't literally try to win a game hoping the other guy will lose his job. But realistically, what happens is that the more I win, the more somebody else loses, or vice versa. The more they win, the more I lose—and that threatens my position.

Yet, when that position is threatened, it's the coaches who come to each other's aid because we understand how hard it is. It is absolutely an amazing phenomenon.

Y ou don't know the true measure of a man until you sit beside him on a bench, like I did for seven years with Terry Holland. You know who he is because you see him in every kind of situation.

The only situation that's probably more dramatic would be one that is life-threatening. If you're in a foxhole with a guy, then you certainly know the true measure of the man. You trust him with your life. But coaching, in my opinion, is the next closest; when you are sitting there having to make spontaneous decisions together.

The dynamics between two friends who happen to coach together are a study in themselves. You learn to respect each other's opinions. You develop non-verbal ways of communicating and you draw from each other the courage to make difficult decisions—always in the best interests of the team.

T hat's the profession. It's day in and day out. You know the true measure of the men you work with and of the life. You can only understand it if you go through it. Coaches' best friends generally live in other towns—because they are coaching elsewhere.

I can count on one hand the number of times that my wife and I have been to dinner or a cookout with friends. For instance, somebody will call my wife and say, "Why don't you and David come over for a cookout on July 4?" Her answer would be, "I'd have to check with his schedule." "What do you mean you'd have to check with his schedule, it's the Fourth of July?" Well, I could be scheduled to be at a camp, or away on a recruiting trip. I've spent Thanksgiving in Alaska and Christmas in Hawaii playing ball with my team. Our lifestyle is different. It's hard for people who don't live it every day to understand. There's a downside to it, but the good far outweighs the bad.

C oaches always do a lot of informal interviewing. As you talk at conventions and meetings you've always got your eye out for people who look the part and people who act the part.

You look at how a person represented his head coach or his school in a particular recruiting battle. Did he do it in an ethical and moral fashion or did he attack you? Did he sell his own program or did he take particular shots at yours? Those are the things that I notice as I'm in the process of doing my job. And when it's time to hire somebody, I take all of those things into consideration.

I think, "I wouldn't hire Coach A because I remember back in 1992 when that nasty situation happened. I wouldn't want him working for me, I know that's in his blood. However, I remember Coach B when we went head to head for a top prospect in 1994 and I came out of it on top. He never tried to take any unnecessary shots." Did a person lose gracefully? You have a tendency to remember those kinds of things. Sometimes some of your greatest adversaries become your greatest friends.

## My Staff

I think a less-experienced head coach, like I was at East Carolina, probably makes his first mistake when feels like he has to do everything. He's not able to delegate. He doesn't trust others to do it the way he wants it done. As an assistant, you don't delegate, you "do." Most coaches become head coaches after they've spent time as an assistant. So you continue coaching as a head coach the same way you did as an assistant. You do.

As an assistant, you do. You make the phone calls. You call the recruits. You watch the tapes. So you take those traits with you to the head coaching position. You are afraid if you don't do it yourself, it won't be done to your satisfaction.

One of the other mistakes that coaches make is that they hire people who are not threats to themselves, because they're not secure enough to hold them off. They don't want some young, energetic, smart, aggressive youngster usurping their authority.

A s you get older and you become more confident—more successful and thus more confident—you begin to understand that you are only as strong as those around you who support you and work with you. That's when you really become at ease with who you are and with your position. You have much more confidence when you quit worrying about others so much.

I t takes a while for that to happen. It's different with every person, but it took me a while to get to that point. I don't think I was ever insecure with who I was, but particularly at East Carolina, I did fall prey to trying to do too much. I wanted to do everything.

I knew what I wanted done and I tried to do it. I didn't give my assistants enough room to develop. As I look back, I couldn't have had a better staff, yet I didn't use them properly. When I look at where they are today, it's incredible that the four of us were together at one time.

My first staff at East Carolina was composed of Eddie Payne, who presently is the head coach at Oregon State University; George Felton, chief assistant at the University of Kentucky; and David Pendergraft, who is currently the director of player personnel with the NBA New Jersey Nets.

T oday I do things differently. I think every head coach has a different approach toward his or her staff, and mine is more of a practical approach. I think you learn by doing. You accomplish by doing. You learn by your mistakes.

I want every assistant I have to be involved in every part of our program. One of my responsibilities to them is to help them develop fully so that they will have a chance to run their own programs some day if they so choose and if they have the opportunity.

I expect all of our coaches to be involved in every recruiting situation, regardless of their race or the prospect's race. I feel very strongly that asking African-American coaches to only recruit minorities is unfair. I ask our staff to sell the university and our basketball program first, and our staff second. I prefer hiring coaches who also recruit, not recruiters who happen to coach.

Far and away the most important ingredients in building a great coaching staff—assuming that all things are equal in terms of knowledge—are that everybody's got a passion for the game; a real love for the athlete himself; and a genuine commitment and loyalty to each other, one coach to another. That's the way you build a staff. If you can find that, you can work the rest of it out.

When you are hiring assistants, sometimes you look for a particular strength, for example, a big-man coach, but I'm big on staff chemistry. If you asked me what is the most important factor in whatever success Wake Forest has had, I would say it's staff chemistry and our ability as a staff to work cohesively and to complement each other. More important than Rodney Rogers, more than Randolph Childress, more than Tim Duncan, more than any one player, are the guys on our staff. We have great continuity and great togetherness and we have complemented each other.

I'm not comfortable in a setting where there is too much formal structure. I prefer having the boundaries of a job defined, but not set in concrete. I like some flexibility. That's what coaching is — being able to adapt.

I want everybody working in every phase. You learn a lot about people once you do it that way. If you narrowly define your roles, things have a tendency to go one of two ways. If I say to my assistant, "Frank Haith, you're in charge of recruiting," I'll find out one of two things about Frank Haith. Either he'll stay in that area and do nothing else, or he will begin to break out of that mold because he wants to be a complete coach.

If he stays in it, then that's all he'll ever be. If he breaks out of what I defined as his job, then I know he wants to be well-rounded as a coach. So I prefer not to box either one of us in.

I prefer to say, "Frank, you head up recruiting, but Ernie Nestor, you help with that. Ernie, you head up game preparation, but Frank, you help with that." I want each of them working in both areas, but you've got to have somebody who's really in charge. However, I don't want an assistant feeling that since someone else is in charge, he has no input in that area.

It's everybody's job. I live that life every day and I think my assistants understand that. I think we're organized, but it might not appear that way to somebody coming in who is a '90s coach.

## My Players

The most important relationship and responsibility at any level of coaching is that of coach–athlete. When I talk about the coach–athlete relationship, I'm talking about the relationship between the entire coaching staff and the athletes, not just my relationship as head coach with the players.

A healthy coach–athlete relationship is vital to the success of any team. It is important in every way — time-consuming, thought-provoking, hands-on caring — and should be at the heart of every decision that is made. It is important in every aspect. Unfortunately, it does not always end up being that way, but that's the way it should be.

I say coach–athlete instead of coach–student-athlete only because, in the pros, there is no student-athlete. But even coaching professionally, the relationship between coach and player should still be far and away the most important. No matter what the level, the basis of every team is the connection between the coach and the player, and between teammates. That's the essence of every successful team.

The amount of time that this relationship takes is probably a greater percentage of a coach's time than you would think. If you only look at the percentage of time that you spend directly involved with your athletes, it may not be that great. But even in game and practice preparation, and looking at the tapes and drawing on the board, you are still coaching. You're still preparing yourself to deal with your athletes. I would say 40 percent of your time is spent dealing either directly or indirectly with your student athletes.

The relationship with your staff occupies a far greater percentage of time because a lot of the areas overlap. You are interacting with your staff not only while you are floor coaching, but in all areas of preparation — from recruiting strategies to travel plans. The relationship with the staff is all-encompassing and it cuts across all lines, but I count that equal in importance to your relationship with your athletes.

I prefer to coach my team much as I coach the coaches. "This is what we've got to do, now everybody pitch in and let's do it." That's true on the court inside the lines. Defensively, you guard your man and one more. It's one of our rules. Offensively, you know what you are capable of doing and you try to do that first. You take care of that first. Then you try to know what your teammate is capable of doing and you try to help him do that.

The same is true off the court, outside the lines. The players know what it takes to be a good team. They know the value of being punctual, of being loyal to each other and to the coaches. They know the value of taking care of their academic responsibilities, of time management, of proper social behavior, of public opinion. Everybody tries to help; they all have a part in it.

I believe in communication. I probably do more explaining than I should. Some people have told me that I tell my players far too much. But that's me. I want to know, so I assume that they want to know. And I think I communicate pretty well with them.

At the college level, players know far more than we give them credit for knowing. Telling them the obvious is almost belittling. I don't feel too comfortable doing that. "If we win this game, we'll win the championship." They know that. I give them credit for knowing that, for being aware.

G uiding your players is like tending a garden. You get the weeds out and you fertilize it. You've got to balance the two every day. You hoe it. You water it. If you let it go unattended, it will absolutely deteriorate on you.

The same thing is true of the human mind and body. You've got to have your finger on the pulse every day and patience is necessary. It may be a process of two steps forward and one step back, or even sometimes two back and one forward, because you lose a little ground. But with daily care and patience, you've got a chance to make up the deficit.

E very team is different. There are no two teams that you can deal with in exactly the same way. You just try to stay on top of things as you go along, try to decide what problems you have, and then deal with them in advance. Preventing problems allows you to spend more time developing your players and your team, rather than repairing situations.

T here is a tape available through the ACC office that is particularly descriptive about the issue of gambling in today's society, as well as in the world of sport. Each year I show my team this tape and invite members of our on-campus security force and the Winston-Salem Police Department to talk about issues in society like gambling, drug involvement, and sexual harassment.

These experts can speak on a personal level about the vulnerability of today's athletes in these different areas. Hopefully, by talking about these issues early on, our athletes will keep themselves out of circumstances that might cause problems for them, our basketball team, and our university.

E very new class brings a different set of problems. In any class, virtually all the players you sign were stars in their own communities. No matter what you say, they're not going to understand that there are six other guys coming in thinking that they're just as good.

Players all think pretty much the same way, "Why can't I be the star? Why can't I be the All-American? Why can't I be the team leader?" It's hard. Identifying a player's role on a team, and having him accept it, gives him the best chance to be successful and gives our team the best chance to reach its potential.

My first recruiting class at Wake Forest was made up of six recruits, one of whom was Marc Blucas, probably the least heralded of the group. He came to us from Girard, a small town in Pennsylvania where, at 6' 3", he had been the starting center. He led his team to the state championship his junior year and they were state runners-up his senior year.

When he arrived on our campus, he was confronted with players like Rodney Rogers and Randolph Childress, each of whom had more athletic ability than Marc. After two years of watching Marc struggle and search, I called him in and we identified some things that he could do better than anyone else on our team, like defending, playmaking, and generally having great court awareness. These were qualities that every good team needs and that our particular team was lacking at the time.

Marc went to work filling the role that I identified for him. He ended up being a starter in his junior and senior seasons and was an invaluable member of both teams.

P layers find their own levels very quickly and then your problems become twofold. You have to deal with those who won the battle, making sure that they don't feel like they're too valuable.

Then you've got to deal with the egos of those who lost the short-term battle and are facing the sudden, stark reality that they're not going to be college stars. They can be good, but they're not going to be stars. You've got to begin to repair their egos by giving them self-worth of a different kind. Identifying important roles, and helping them fill these roles, gives them the best chance to succeed.

I assign roommates the first year because I know more about my players than they know about themselves at that point, and I have executive veto power from then on. But generally, I don't get involved much after the first year. The first year is the most important and they need to get off to a good start. Being paired with a responsible roommate is crucial to every freshman's happiness.

They also need to be with somebody who is on virtually the same schedule they're on. You don't need a basketball player rooming with a football player, because when the football season's over—and the football player's ready to relax—basketball's under way and the basketball player needs quiet. So you don't want to mix apples and oranges the first year.

I do want them to have some flexibility after the first year, however. After that year, everybody knows enough about themselves that they're not likely to pick a bad roommate. But still I want to be involved in the process.

Coaching a superstar-type player presents additional challenges. I've had the opportunity to coach two players—Ralph Sampson at Virginia and Tim Duncan at Wake Forest—who fell into that category. The common denominator between those two was that they were extraordinarily talented people who really wanted to be treated like everybody else. They rarely asked for anything exceptional or different—in fact, they asked far less than normal players would ask. They made it easy on us, on me.

It can be a real problem for a team if you've got some-body who is different and knows it and wants to be treated that way. At some point, you have to come to grips with the fact that you can't bend any further in that direction because it becomes divisive.

I t helps when a star is the first guy to practice and the last one to leave. He needs to be the hardest worker. He needs to be the leader, the most devoted. He has the most to lose, as well as the most to gain. He needs to understand that the team can be only as strong as its weakest member. He needs to understand that he is only as good as those around him. He needs to understand that there must be a strong link be-tween himself, his teammates, and the coaching staff.

All these things need to come together, and if you are pro-active with it, you try to deal with it in advance as you go along. It's not a one-time sit-down session. It's done every day. It's making sure that he follows the same guidelines as everybody else. If your rule is no hats in the office and he comes in with a hat on, you tell him to take it off. He has to expect that. The basis of every good team is strong discipline, and having the discipline to take your hat off in the office, if that is the rule, is important.

I think in a really successful program you'll treat every-body as nearly alike as you can. But they're not all the same. Each one has different abilities and needs as players and as people. They all deserve something different. Though I try to treat them all fairly, I don't feel a need to treat each one exactly the same. You try to treat each person as they de-serve to be treated. I think that's the way to do it.

I'm not a great believer in a set of rules. I don't print and hand out the "ten commandments of basketball." I think those things box you in sometimes. Having set rules takes away some of your flexibility as a coach. Every situation has its own set of circumstances. We try to deal with each instance as it comes up, and on its own merits. Attacking situations this way allows you not to have too many rules.

I t's been said that a parent's idea of who a coach should play is the four best players on the team, plus his or her child. College parents may think that, but conveying that to the college coach is difficult. We don't see them a lot. Occasionally you have pressure from parents, but it's not as pronounced as it is at the high school or the youth level. The youth level is where you really have problems—and where the problems begin. Coaches and parents don't interact as much at the college level.

## The Administration

A good relationship with your bosses, regardless of the level, is crucial to a coach's success. In the last decade, I've seen a place like Wake Forest that has always prided itself on being small, warm, and personal, become more corporate. It's leaning heavily toward a more corporate approach to things now. That's not necessarily bad, but it does require an adjustment for those of us who came up in a different era.

In a way, it's somewhat sad, because one of the real attractions of this university is its ability to foster great relationships. It's hard to do that with voice mail and excessive memos and faxes and Fed Ex's and other modern ways of communicating.

I've made an effort, and I think the administration has pretty much responded, to keep our relationship on a personal level. I'm most comfortable in an atmosphere of trust:

"You know what I'm doing. Let's not be too detailed in our contracts and let me do my job. I promise you I'll do it every day and, in return, I know you're going to fulfill the promises that you've made me from a contractual standpoint."

Perhaps you have a little more flexibility in a private institution than in a public institution, but there are probably not as many differences as people might think. I saw my salary printed (though incorrectly) in the paper a while back when I didn't think that was possible. I thought that happened only at public schools. But when you're at a private school, you don't feel like the public is watching everything you do in quite the same way as when you're at a state school.

When your school is aligned athletically with a conference, I think you give up a lot of that flexibility. Leagues are very homogeneous in the way they think and the way they act. It is important that the lines of communication always be open between each university and the conference office, for it is your voice nationally.

## The Media

I 've found the best way to deal with the media is straightforwardly and honestly. I think they value those qualities the most—as well as the head coach's availability. I've tried to be available. I don't know whether they'd agree that I have or not, but I feel like my door's always open to them. I don't hold a press conference at a regularly assigned time, but invariably they get me sometime before every game.

The league has tried to help with media access by setting up a weekly 10-minute teleconference for each coach. Although most reporters take part, the individual media outlets still come back to you for their own approach. People don't want to ask questions publicly because then everybody will have their slant, so you end up doing interviews several times and answering the same questions over and over again anyway.

O ur television show right now is easy for me because I'm not responsible for anything except showing up and giving them ideas on what the show should contain. There's very little preparation required on my part. We do my portion of the show at the site of the games. It's a lot easier than it used to be, when the taping occurred on Sunday morning in High Point. It used to take two hours to do a half-hour show, plus driving time. Now it's less time-consuming and more compatible with my busy schedule.

## The Fans

T he radio call-in show is a bittersweet thing. If you win, everybody calls in to tell you how well you're doing and if you lose, everybody tells you what you should've done. So I've tried to become the master of deflection.

I don't care what they ask me, I give them a certain answer. Then I talk a fair amount of time about every single question, which cuts down on the number of calls you get in the hour. We've basically got a regular group of callers, but occasionally you'll hear from somebody different. I think the show's important because it puts you in touch with the people who care the most. Some of them are critical, but they are critical only because they care.

It's the same as dealing with the media. I think making yourself available has a way of endearing you to people. You can't like somebody you don't know. I want people to know who I am. I don't want to force myself on anybody, but if they want to know who I am, I want to make that possible.

I continue to remind myself that when fans attack you verbally, it's because they care. I don't necessarily believe that if they pay their dollar they can say anything they want to say. But I do understand that generally, when they write critical letters—even overly critical letters that at times are irrational in their expectations and beliefs—it's because they care. As a coach, my job is to help them understand and, in part, to help them become less emotional, less personal, and more reasonable in their expectations.

I try to answer every letter, and that's very, very time consuming. A lot of coaches don't do that. I can't say that I answer every one individually, but I try.

At the beginning of the year—and I try to do this before I know what kind of season we're going to have—I'll write two letters that I will basically use for the year. One says, "Thank you for your letter. I'm proud of our team, too. I hope we continue to improve."

Then I'll write the opposite. I'll write a letter that says something like, "I'm sorry we're not playing up to your expectations. I know we haven't performed well of late, but I hope that before the end of the year we'll turn around and begin to make more progress."

I always save a paragraph in each letter to make it personal. For instance, if the writer questioned a particular coaching decision, then I'll address the specific situation. It lets them know that I did read their letter, because I feel if they write me, then they deserve an answer if the letter calls for an answer.

Once I answer, it brings closure to the situation. I don't want to hold a person's letter against him or her forever. I want to let it go. Again, I try to remember that they wrote the letter because they cared and I care, too. We may come at a situation from different slants, but we both care.

I think booster clubs, such as the Deacon Club, have a right to expect maximum effort. They have a right to expect the coach to set a great example for himself, for his team, for the university, and for them. They should expect him to operate his program with the highest moral ethics at all times, to make good moral and ethical decisions, and to lead in an aggressive, but always a respectful, manner. You need to be respectful of others and show great pride in the university that you are working for and in its constituents.

## Tradition

I think your high moments in coaching transcend championships. After our first ACC championship, I remember talking to my team in the locker room right after the game. I was holding the ACC championship trophy in my hand and I said, "You know, this trophy is not ours unto ourselves. This trophy belongs to the university, to every player that's ever played and put on a Wake Forest uniform—whether they played for me or before me—to everybody who helped build and get us to this moment, and to those who sacrificed before so that we could play today."

I really do believe that, because Wake Forest, like most universities, has experienced some hard times athletically and some great times. A great foundation and a great heritage—it takes all of those things coming together at one time to make a great moment.

It doesn't happen just with a certain Randolph Childress shot at the buzzer that wins the tournament for you. That shot alone did not win the tournament. All the things that went before that got you to that moment—they're what make the moment possible.

# Chapter 7

# Recruiting — You Just Can't Take It Personally

*"In every situation somebody different is pushing the critical decision button. When in doubt, recruit the player."*

Recruiting is not unlike selling. You are going to get told "no" more than you are going to be told "yes" — you just can't take it personally. When I first got started, I let rejections bother me. "How could anybody tell me no? How could they not want to play for me?" It hurt my feelings. You gradually get past that, but you still subconsciously ask yourself, "How could anybody be more committed to coaching and to players than I am? Does he see something that I don't see?" You get told no enough that you eventually understand that's not it, and you learn to move on.

The summer camps are the beginning point for recruiting. The camp scene now has changed. They've actually gone more corporate than they are individual. Nike runs its own camp and Adidas runs its own camp. The private camps like Five-Star are still in existence, but they don't corner quite the talent market that they once did, because athletes still have to pay to go to those camps and the weekly rate has really gone up.

There was a period of time when Nike and the corporate camps could pay for campers to come. But the NCAA essentially said that they cannot do that, so presumably everybody who goes, pays. But the camps can charge whatever they want, and the corporate ones can charge a much smaller fee than the private camps.

P robably the greatest vehicles for exposure right now are the summer camps and AAU tournaments. In a way, that's a shame. I hold to the belief that the best measure of talent is found in the summers, when the best players go against each other. Still, I believe that the high school coach should be in control of his player's recruitment and that freeing the athlete to play all over the country for others—national camps, AAU tournaments—only opens the door for unsavory characters to get their hooks into great young players. The National Collegiate Athletic Association (NCAA) and the National Association of Basketball Coaches (NABC) in conjunction with USA Basketball are presently studying the situation.

Athletes should also be seen in a more structured environment—at their own schools, with their own coaches, in their own systems. I want to see how they interact in both places. Generally, high school coaches play a fairly big role in their players' recruitment. Of course it varies, but when we've been successful, it's been when there was great influence from the parents and the high school coach at the same time. I prefer that to dealing with someone outside the natural recruiting process. I'm just not going to recruit that way.

There are some high school coaches who send letters every year saying, "This is my player and you need to come look at him"—and those are valuable. However, I think generally, the relationships that end up producing results are those that we generate or initiate.

I t wasn't hard for me going from being a high school coach, where you don't have to recruit, to college where recruiting is everything. Recruiting has never been a problem for me. I don't know if I do it well or not, but I feel confident in our system and the results that we have produced. Recruiting is basically getting to know people and getting them to trust you.

Certainly, there are important evaluations that have to be made—you've got to make some sort of judgment about the value of a player athletically and how he'd fit into your system.

But, in fact, you do that at the high school level as you try to put your team together. I knew exactly how Marshall Ashford fit in with Billy Byrd as teammates at Durham High School, for instance. So I don't think it's hard to do. Recruiting is really about getting to know people and letting them get to know you and feel comfortable with you.

W hen I'm recruiting, I always look for both athletic ability and someone who will fit in with the team. The first step is deciding what your needs are. You need to be able to project a year or two ahead and determine where your team might be weak. Then being able to find the raw talent is not difficult. If you need a low-post center, you can find a low-post center in this country.

It's when you add all of the extra factors that it becomes more difficult. For instance, if you say that you need a low-post center who's got great grades, has no social baggage, is a great kid, comes from a good, two-parent family, has a deep and abiding appreciation for academics, and wants to get his degree—now you've limited yourself quite a bit. But yet that's the type of player, student, and person we all want.

I n some cases you end up sacrificing athletic ability for enhanced qualities in other areas, like academic acumen or
the desire and ability to be successful. You might take someone who's got an upside that you feel is limitless, but you
begin sacrificing certain things. You may take one step less
speed for three-tenths of a point on the GPA.

J ust finding a "player" is not difficult. Once you determine
your needs, then you can begin to investigate the
prospects — their personal lives and what their motives might
be for coming to a place like Wake Forest — and try to put
the two together. For example, I go over recruiting lists every
day and if I can't visualize in my mind why a certain kid
should come to Wake Forest, there's no way I can talk him
into coming. If I can't convince *myself*, then you know I can't
convince *him*.

T he most memorable recruiting trip I can remember occurred when we were at the height of our program at
Virginia. Ralph Sampson was a senior and getting ready to
graduate that year. I was recruiting Tom Sheehey, who lived
in Rochester, New York. I had made an untold number of
trips up there and everything had come down to his last official visit, which was to Virginia.

On that same weekend, we were going to have three
players from New York City — Henry Dalrymple, Olden
Polynice and Kenny Smith — visit UVA along with Tom Sheehey. An alumnus had loaned us a corporate jet and I left
town about 1:00 a.m. and flew to Rochester, getting in about
3:00 a.m.

Back in the early '80s, buffalo wings were just becoming
popular, and every time I would go to Rochester, Tom Sheehey would take me to a restaurant that had his favorite
wings. In that era, you were allowed to eat with recruits, but

not pay for their food. Since one of the things you try to do as a recruiter is make people feel at home, I had called the restaurant and asked if they could have a big pan of wings ready for me to pick up very early in the morning. My idea was that I'd take them back to Charlottesville with us and when we got there and had our big weekend party, I'd bring those chicken wings out and just sweep him off his feet.

So soon after arriving in Rochester around 3:00 a.m., I picked up a huge pan of wings and put them on the plane. I was supposed to pick up Tom at 6:00 a.m. because we had to fly on to New York City and pick up the other three recruits and get back to Charlottesville by 10:00 a.m. It was our plan for the four recruits to visit a class that morning at UVA.

Just as daylight was beginning to break, my taxi, driven by a very old driver, pulled into the Sheehey's driveway. I saw the lights on, so I knew everything was okay.

I knocked on the door and Tom's father, who was an ophthalmologist, answered and said, "Oh yeah, Tom's ready. He'll be right down." His mother came out and we chatted a minute. Then Tom came dragging out, looking as if he'd only been awake about 15 minutes.

We said our goodbyes and I told his folks that we would take good care of him and for them not to worry.

As the cab driver started backing out of the driveway, all of a sudden we were startled by loud yelping sounds. The cab driver had run over the Sheehey's dog on the way out. He hit the dog that had grown up with Tom, the dog that was almost the same age — sixteen — as Tom was. Tom shouted, "Oh, you hit my dog! You hit my dog!" and jumped out of the cab and grabbed the dog. As he picked up the dog, the dog snapped at him, biting his arm, and all of a sudden, blood started gushing everywhere.

I'm embarrassed to admit that my first thought was, "There goes my recruit." I wasn't worried about the dog or about Tom's arm. I was worried about myself and Virginia. I jumped out of the car and ran to his father and said, "Doc, just wrap his arm up. We've got one of the best medical schools in the country in Charlottesville. Let's get him down there and I'll get him taken care of." I didn't want to short-circuit the visit.

Tom's arm was bleeding quite a lot, but his mother was a nurse and they bandaged it up as best as they could and I went ahead and called Terry Holland at his house — it was still just six-thirty in the morning — and told him to have a doctor ready.

With Tom's arm elevated so that it wouldn't bleed any more, we flew off to pick up the other three kids at a small airport outside Manhattan. All of them knew each other because they had played on the same summer league team together.

The three got in the plane and saw Tom's arm — by then the blood had come through the bandage — and they were in semi-shock and could hardly speak. These were kids who had never flown on a small plane before and their apprehension showed. We finally got back to Charlottesville and actually ended up having a great weekend. We signed two of them — Sheehey and Polynice — and the chicken wings were a hit! Kelly, the dog, lived another year!


I think for a place like Wake Forest, Prop 48 has made recruiting a little bit easier because it's gotten the scores closer to what the university would normally take. You don't really have to worry about kids going to other schools just because we can't take them, because the minimum scores are the same for everybody. Our admissions people have worked pretty well with us. We can't get every prospect that we want, but I can generally get one in a year with SAT scores lower than the standard university requirement.

So it's helped. We get a little better student, but we can't fool ourselves. The high schools know that their students have to have an 820 SAT score and a 2.5 grade-point average and they will teach to that level. In most cases, the student-athletes will get what they need to qualify.

In an ideal world, we would see standards tightened even before kids get to high school. If we asked more of our students, even before they got to high school, then it would make the job of the high school counselors, coaches, and teachers easier. That, in turn, would make our jobs more realistic—but that's probably not going to happen. The public schools in some places are just not equipped to handle those kinds of situations.

S ome coaches have argued that Prop 48 is hurting minority students rather than helping them, but I don't agree with that. True, not all students will make it. But regardless of what the standards are, there will be some students who fail to qualify. In the first few years of Prop 48, I did feel bad, because students weren't given enough notice. However, now we've gone through almost a whole decade of Prop 48 and Prop 16, and students and educators have been given enough notice.

Once the generation of kids who are now qualifying under Prop 48 become parents, they'll know, and they'll get their kids ready. Right now, a lot of the problem lies with uninformed parents.

T o say that we're depriving somebody of an education is not accurate. Youngsters deprived themselves by not studying when they were young. Certainly, some of them were disadvantaged early because they came from a single-parent home, or a no-parent home, or they were indigent, and I understand all that; but a sports program can't be all things to all people. I think the real travesty is that we don't have enough leaders in most communities to structure, discipline, and motivate these youngsters so that there are fewer disappointments. It is paramount that we should always offer the opportunity—and then support and assist every student who qualifies.

M aybe we've reached the point that we must say that college is not for everybody. We're the only country in the world that says everybody's got to go to college to be successful. That's not true. There are lots of successful people, even in our country, who never went to college. College is not for everyone—just like everyone can't go into politics, everyone can't be a lawyer, everyone can't be an electrician or a machinist. Everybody has different talents and just because a person doesn't go to college or doesn't finish college doesn't mean that he or she has no worth. Everybody has worth—it's just that you find it in different places and in different ways.

I n some of the better athletic neighborhoods in America, the premise exists that the way out of the neighborhood is with a basketball in your hand, high-flying as you slam dunk it. That's in direct conflict with the notion that four years of college and a diploma give you the best chance for years of happiness and success and self-sufficiency.

The problem that coaches face is trying to convince these kids that they can have both, because generally when they get here, they have had only one or the other. We've got to balance their lives with the ingredient they need most.

We've got to catch them up. In Tim Duncan's case, we had to catch up his athletic side. He came from a private Episcopal school in St. Croix and he was fine academically. So the catching up is not always one-sided, although more commonly, students need help academically.

T he story of Tim Duncan's recruitment is an interesting one. One of my former players came back from the Caribbean and told me that he'd seen a player down there who was very good but he didn't know his name or remember on which island he had seen him. So I put one of my crack assistants on chasing him down, and in just two days he had Tim's name, telephone number, and address. I got him on the phone and made an appointment with him in St. Croix.

I went down and watched him play, and was delighted that he was as big as I'd heard (6' 10") and that he was highly skilled. My home visit with him was scheduled for that evening.

I knocked on the door and his dad greeted me. He invited me in and told me that Tim was in the living room. I walked in and Tim was sitting on the floor in a relatively small room, leaning up against the couch. It was October, and the television was on, tuned to an NFL game — the Bears were playing somebody — and he had his eyes glued to the TV set. I tried to talk to him a little bit but there was not a great deal of conversation and I kept thinking, "Gosh, I'm not getting anywhere here."

I hated to just say, "Would you please turn off the TV so we can talk," but I really felt that he was being somewhat rude and I was determined not to come all that distance without getting a good shot at him. I decided that the easiest way to do that, short of cutting off the TV myself, was to sit down next to the TV with my back to the wall, so that he was facing not only the TV, but me, as I talked to him about recruiting.

I remember his dad walked in about halfway through the conversation and just smiled and laughed and walked back out. I actually gave Tim my spiel with the TV on and with him looking almost exclusively at the TV, although occasionally, if I'd ask him something, he'd look at me.

I remember thinking about halfway through my presentation to him that this kid wasn't hearing anything I was saying and that I was wasting my time. When I got through, the game was over and the TV was turned off and I decided to test him.

I started asking him questions like, "What do you think about our academic program?" and he was able to spit back to me, virtually verbatim, everything I had told him. I was amazed. It was one of the few times that I had ever been in a situation like that.

Because of the way I am, I can only do one thing well at a time—and then sometimes I don't even do that well. But here was a kid who, at 16 years old, was able to watch TV and listen to a stranger at the same time and in general, do pretty well. I've never forgotten that.

I know him better now—and I now realize it was his way of delaying an answer until he'd had time to think about things or holding me at bay until he was ready to deal with the issue. It's an effective tactic, and one that he utilizes even today.


C arl Tacy taught me that in every situation somebody different is pushing the critical decision button. If you ever get into a recruiting situation and you can't tell whether it's the player, a parent, the coach, or somebody in the community—always recruit the player.

You've got to honor all of these people, but you've got to spend your time on the one who's going to push the right button. When in doubt, recruit the player.

# Chapter 8

# A Sense of Balance

*"The end is not the trophy."*

O ne of the most important things in coaching is learning balance. Those of us who have lasted the longest have probably learned to achieve some sort of balance. Take Dean Smith; he lasted as long as he did because he's a great coach but just as important, he had found a sense of balance somewhere. I don't know where it was with him because I don't really know him. But I am sure that he had this element of control in his life, otherwise the tremendous highs and lows would have taken their toll much earlier in his career. Now, it seems, the balance has been lost due to the many dmeands placed upon him beyond basketball.

D ean Smith's retirement brought into focus my own coaching mortality because he was somebody who I thought would coach forever, and I really mean *forever*. How could he not be the coach for the University of North Carolina?

The fact that he stepped aside only one week before practice and his 37th year as head coach started, only motivates me more. Learning of Dean's retirement made clear in my mind that I would not coach forever, either. Thus, I want to make the very best of every moment that I do have.

W hen I heard the news of his retirement and found out that it was true, the first sensation that I felt was real sadness, because I know how deeply he cares about college basketball and how much he has meant to our game. It's going to be a great loss for those of us who learned from him.

I also felt a sense of sadness for the Atlantic Coast Conference because he's been very much a part of our league almost since its inception. My thoughts then quickly turned to my own coaching career because an event like that causes you to reflect upon the opportunity you have to affect lives.

T hrough the years, people have asked me how long Dean Smith would coach and I had always answered one of two ways: forever, or as long as he wants. And when I said forever, that's what I meant. When I said that, I could never imagine him not coaching. But now that "forever" has come, it makes us realize that none of us is going to coach forever.

Dean Smith is the greatest competitor as a coach that I have ever faced. His departure from the coaching ranks leaves a void that can never be filled by any one person. As a profession, we coaches must work very hard to fill the vacuum.

D ean Smith, to my way of thinking, was and is the best basketball coach of all time by any standard you want to set—except national championships. He's stood the test of time and he's stayed at one university. He's coached in the most highly publicized leagues in the country, and he's done it with great grace and dignity. His programs have always been operated at the very highest level, and his teams have always been absolutely prepared.

H aving had the chance to coach against him has helped to make me a better coach, because only when coaching against a man like that do you realize the extent to which you must be prepared and the amount of talent you must have to offset his teams and the efficiency of his teams. He brought out the best in everyone.

It was recently pointed out that since I've been in the league for 20 years, I probably have been paired against him more than any other coach. It's been a real joy and an honor to coach against him and to coach in the same league with him.

M en like Dean feed off the game itself, and when the activities and requirements of the job take more of their time than the game, they start to question whether it's really what they want to do. Most of us tolerate the off-court duties just so we can get to the court.

In Dean's case, it's likely that the percentage of time spent away from the game had become overwhelming and the imbalance had affected his feelings about his job. That's sad, because the profession itself has had the tendency to go in that direction, particularly in the last five to ten years.

In a way, coaches are at fault, too. At the highest level, coaches are paid well for their expertise and, as financial packages have risen, so have the demands upon a coach's time. With the financial rewards come expectations, many of which don't really have anything to do with coaching and teaching. I'm not blaming the system, that's just the way things are right now. At some point we need to ease up a bit so that we can find the time to do what we enjoy most — coaching — without feeling so much external pressure.

O ne thing that Dean did, which is very, very important, was to put his program in a position so that when he walked away from it, the program could sustain itself or perhaps even get better. He left the blocks of a very solid foundation in place and he could walk away knowing that the team was well prepared to have a great year. From that standpoint, he didn't feel a need to stay.

Y ou have to have balance in all areas of your life. When my sons were growing up, it was hard to juggle schedules, especially all of our various games and practices. I did as well as I possibly could, but Lynn did a better job. She did a great job of dividing her time almost equally among the three of us and managed to give us each as much attention as she could.

She really fell in love with watching our sons play and coach. During the last few years, when Lane coached and Ryan played, she even missed some of the Wake Forest games in order to watch them. But that was fine with me, because it was very exciting for her to see them perform. I tried to see as many of their games as I could, but I was much more limited, since our seasons are concurrent.

I don't believe that a coach's wife has to be particularly knowledgeable about his sport or sports. In fact, sometimes I think less knowledgeable is better because, as a couple, you don't feel compelled to talk about it each night. Lynn is interested, but she's not demanding in terms of having to know everything that's going on with my team.

She's very supportive, but we don't have to talk about everything that happened that day in the office, or in practice, or about why I made a certain decision in a game. That's not part of our lives. She can tell how things went just by how I act when I get home. She adjusts to my moods naturally.

We have our own life when I get home, so I don't think it's absolutely necessary to have a wife be overly involved—

although I don't think it's wrong for them to be that way either. But in my case, I want to leave my work at the office as much as possible.

I don't always do a good job of that and if you've got the added responsibility of sharing everything with your wife when you get home, then you never get away from it. Lynn has been great—she knows when to say when.

The boys are different. They can't get enough of it. They are like sponges. They soak everything in. Basketball has been a big part of their lives, all of their lives, and it's hard for them to get away from it. My fondest hope for them is not only that they find happiness in it, but that they also find balance. Right now there is little balance in their lives. That's all they do. But I think they will find it in time.

Lane is beginning to understand that there needs to be some time away from basketball, time doing other things. Ryan hasn't gotten to that point yet. He still hasn't had enough of it.

There's no question that it took me quite a while to get to that point. I was consumed with basketball almost to a fault. People can talk to you about the need for balance in your life all they want, but until you acknowledge the imbalance yourself, you won't be able to resolve it.

You need to strike a balance between wanting to win and understanding that playing college ball is a learning process and, above all, a game. You've got to walk the walk that you talk. Basketball seasons are long. You are teaching and coaching every day. The kids are looking around all the time and they see you. If you tell them one thing and you do another, they know.

S ome people say that they're afraid to lose, and that fear spurs them to be great. I don't necessarily believe that, because being afraid to lose can keep you from being relaxed. You start worrying about the wrong things. You worry about the effects of losing and start envisioning the big real estate signs in front of your house.

O ther people are afraid to win, because winning brings its own set of pressures. With winning comes greater responsibility and greater expectations. The more you win, the more everyone expects. With a higher level of expectation comes the possibility for greater disappointment. One has a tendency to work on the other.

W e get afraid of our own success. We ride it out as long as it continues, and then when it begins to level off, we try to regroup, rebuild, reload, and go again to see if we can get a little further this time.

In fact, you shouldn't be worried about the end results so much. You should be concerned only with the experience of growing and improving. Then the fear of winning or losing would be far less important.

S uccess raises the question, "How much is enough?" How many lives must you affect in order to feel successful? If you're a business person, how much money must you make? If you're a lawyer, how many cases must you win? If you are a doctor, how many diseases must you cure? If you are a coach, how many championships will satisfy you?

The obvious answer is that there is no answer—it's open-ended. If you bank your life on what the end result might be, you'll always end up dissatisfied.

At Wake Forest we won two ACC Tournament championships in a row ('93–'94 and '94–'95), yet going into the '95–'96 season, I wanted to win another one. Two wasn't enough.

Although Wake Forest had not won consecutive championships for 33 years—nor had any league team done so since the University of North Carolina in the early 1980s—two weren't enough for me. I wanted to try for another one.I couldn't be afraid to try.

There are certainly more demands on my time since those championships. There is more of everything. There are more autographs to sign, more speeches to make, maybe more pressure—but I had to find a way to handle it all. Though demanding, everything else paled against the needs of my team as we prepared ourselves for a third championship run.

Learn to live with a sense of fearlessness. Don't be afraid. Learn to do your best and let it rest. That's important in all walks of life, but particularly for a coach or a competitor. You compete for the experience that goes with it, not for the plaque at the end. The end is not the trophy.

It can't be, because you can never win enough trophies to satisfy you. The satisfaction has to be in the experience of the competition itself. We won two ACC championships in a row and I can't tell you the final score of either game. I can tell you that we played North Carolina the first year and Georgia Tech the second, but I can't tell you the score of either game.

I can, however, tell you in detail about the games themselves. I can tell you in detail about the events leading up to those games. The hard work and countless hours of preparation far outweighed any final scores or championship.

That's a tremendous lesson for coaches to learn—for *people* to learn, because it goes beyond coaching. I really don't think that there's ever enough to satisfy anybody. No matter what "it" is, there's always another one out there to get. What you're doing today has to be enough for you. You've got to enjoy today. A championship is nice, but the best thing is the experience of getting there and the satisfaction you feel in seeing everything come together. The road to a championship is full of great memories, but so is the road to a break-even season if everyone gives championship effort.

T he moments in coaching that people want to know about are moments that occur during the games or at the end of a game when the championship is secure. "What did you feel like?" "What was it like when you went through it?" Or, "What's it like in the huddle?" "Who was your key player?"—those kinds of things.

Those things are like the final exam, but the preparation for the final exam is really far more important—and easier for me to remember—than the exam itself.

T he chase is more important than the catch. You chase the fish. You fish endless numbers of hours to hook one marlin. Well, the marlin is great and it's a rewarding catch, but if you don't reel one in, you still had a good time. That really is what's important. If you don't realize that, you'll always end up unhappy, unsatisfied, and unfulfilled.

I 've got a book that I shared with my team last year called *The Precious Present*. I read it to my team almost in classroom fashion one afternoon. It's a very short book—the story of a young boy searching for happiness. He meets a man who tells him about something called "the precious present." The man says that it is the best present anyone can receive and tells him that one day it will come to him.

So the boy starts looking. On each birthday he opens all his gifts looking for the precious present, but he can't find it. Christmas comes and he looks for the precious present, but can't find it. He becomes fanatical about it.

The years go by and the two meet again and the unhappy young man asks again where the precious present can be found. The old man says that he doesn't have the power to tell him, that only the young man has the power to make himself happy. By the end of the story it becomes obvious to the young man that the precious present is the *now*, it is not found in the past or in the future. It's learning to live now and enjoy today and not be anxious about tomorrow or fretful about yesterday. Only by understanding the real meaning of the precious present can any of us hope to be truly happy. That's a wonderful lesson for all of us.

It's a particularly important lesson for basketball teams who have a lot expected of them. You start off practicing in the middle of October and everybody's full of energy and enthusiasm and nobody's made any mistakes. All of a sudden, in your own mind you're the champion, but the championship's not played until April — and that's not good.

Eventually you either find balance or the imbalance in your life will become a disease and destroy you. The intensity will actually become a negative and you have to correct it and control it. I never did find that sense of balance while coaching in high school. It was probably sometime during my Virginia years — sometime in my early forties — that I began to look at myself and say, "You know, you can accomplish just as much doing it a different way."

I made both psychological and physical changes. Psychologically I said to myself, "You need other things to keep you fresh, to help you appreciate what you've got. You've got to have some balance in your life." A person has to experience "no" to truly appreciate "yes," and experience being poor to appreciate being rich.

I've always been physically active, but I really stepped up my activity about the time I got to Virginia. When you approach 40, it's time to put up or shut up. You really have to go to work or your body's going to fall apart. Physical activity was one of the ways I found balance.

Since then, I always plan each day by investing in myself both physically and mentally, which means taking an hour or two for exercise and/or private or quiet time—time for myself.

I run and play tennis. My best ideas come to me while I'm running. Sometimes I'm amazed I don't get run over because I get into a world of my own out there and nothing matters. When playing tennis, nothing matters. I play competitive tennis for exercise. I only count wins and losses during basketball season. A lot of people worry about the wins and losses in recreational activity, but I don't. I just play. It's a tremendous release.

You balance your life in the same way you balance your money when you get your paycheck. You divide it up—so much for rent, so much for food, so much for gas, so much for utilities, so much for your church, and then so much for yourself.

Many people say you should take out the portion for yourself first because if you don't, there won't be anything left, and I agree with that. I do the same thing with my time, my mind, and my body. I make sure I have that hour a day because it's all too easy to schedule something into that time. Rarely will I give up "my time."

I don't feel good if I don't have it. I don't feel capable of doing all the other things that I'm asked to do. It's an important time for me.

W hen I began to balance my personal life, I changed the way I was coaching a bit, too. As a high school coach and early in my college coaching career, I was a very emotional kind of coach. I still am, but I try to show my emotions less.

Controlling my emotions helps me coach from balance. The highs and lows that you experience are just that. Eventually you've always got to come back to center. You come up to center after a loss or come down after a win.

I try to coach the two hours of my practices that way. "This drill may not be great, but the next one will be really good." Somewhere, in between the two extremes, there's some balance. You try to always keep things on an incline, and that helps as well.

O ne of the hardest things for me as a coach was learning to get over losses. I came face to face with that when I was at Virginia, and I still have a hard time with it. All through high school I faced it as a player. We'd lose a game and I was distraught for days. As a young coach I was awful for days. At Wake Forest, I was terrible; at East Carolina, even worse.

When I was at Virginia, I took note of Tom Landry and Don Shula, two of the NFL's most successful coaches. They were not only successful, but they had been at the top for a long time. I was impressed with how they handled winning and losing; they always seemed to be in balance.

I was once offered a job by Rick Pitino, who was head coach of the New York Knicks at the time. In part of the interview I said to him, "Rick, it would seem to me that the hardest thing about coaching in the pros is the number of games in a season. How can you come back so quickly after a loss?" He said that there was no time to reflect on yesterday, and that you had to quickly turn your attention to the preparation for the next game. He was emphatic that he would never hire a coach who lived in the past.

The fact that you could play 100+ games a year really made an impression. You could actually lose four games in a ten-day period! It is hard to keep your sense of balance there. For those who can, it's extraordinary.

There's only so much emotion that anyone can muster, and you've got to be able to draw your energy from other areas. You have to calculate how much energy you have. We all have different levels of energy. Using all our reserves in one outing leaves us little to draw upon when we need it most. I look at coaching as a long distance race and not as a sprint to the finish line.

First of all, you have to have enough energy to get to the finish line, and when you get there, you've got to be strong. Emotion, though it generates a lot of energy and a lot of short-term results, is hard to sustain over the long haul. There's got to be something left — skill, ability, coaching acumen or the will to win. Whatever it is, there's got to be something to get you over the line.

Too often, winning seems to cause slippage. What happens is that you begin to get your program in place and everybody starts to feel comfortable with what you are achieving. Slippage can occur at any level, from little league through middle or high school coaching, on up to the NBA. We're all vulnerable to slippage.

As you become comfortable and more entrenched in what you are doing, and as you begin to experience success and begin to feel better about yourself, you become a victim of your own success. You follow certain trends. You form certain habits.

For instance, you practice the same way. A lot of it is subconscious. You may not intentionally do it, but you fall into the trap of, "Listen, we practiced like this last time, so it must be good for this team." As a coach, you can lose sight of things and you need to ask, "Yeah, we practiced that way and we won that game and it was good for *that* team *then*, but how do *we* get better *now*?"

When you practice the same way, you stay at the same level, and then gradually the ground around you begins to erode. Boredom sets in. You don't keep yourself stimulated, and if you're not stimulated, you don't grow. It's almost like running on a treadmill.

You continue to do the same things schematically the same way. You practice the same amount of time, at the same time, in the same way. You practice the same drills, the same shots, the same offenses, the same defenses. You look at tape the same number of minutes. Everything becomes the "same old thing." And you experience no growth.

When that happens, boredom sets in and that's when slippage occurs. No longer can you hold your ground —in fact, you actually lose ground. Once that occurs, you almost free fall until you hit bottom, and then you have to build back. Coming back is not that difficult because you've already got a base for success, but stopping the free fall in mid-air is hard.

Additionally, if you don't continue to improve while others do, then the gap between you and your opponents widens and becomes difficult to overcome.

T hat happened to our Wake Forest team in 1996–97. We were good, very good. We were on a 13-game winning streak and then, all of a sudden, we lost a game. And the confidence that we'd worked 13 games to build began to crack — just a chip. You don't really worry, because you figure that if you win two or three more games, you will get it back.

But then we lost another one, and we started to wonder. Other teams focused on how to beat our team and we didn't counteract that. Instead of attacking our problems, we became passive in our preparations.

S lippage is one of the things that successful people have to really be wary of. You must always be alert for its signs. You don't always know whether it's complacency or boredom or fear. Those things you can feel, but can't see, are the hardest things to deal with. You know something's wrong, yet you are a bit reluctant to dive into it, to take it on.

W inning covers up the real you. Are we getting better? Winning covers that up. Sometimes you can lose and still be very pleased with yourself because you know you are getting better. But winning can have the reverse effect — it can cover up the fact that you're not getting better. It takes a really discerning eye to be able to see that. You really need to be constructively critical of your team.

C oaches, like anyone, can be susceptible to "the disease of self." You become too enthralled with your own person. You do things for the wrong reasons. Coaches start out saying, "How do I build my resumé?" "How do I win as many games as I can, as many championships as I can?" "How can I win coach of the year honors as many times as I can?" Those are ways to get ahead, but they are the wrong reasons for coaching.

If people coach for the wrong reasons, eventually those reasons become self-destructive and will eat you up. You'll begin to take yourself too seriously, particularly if you attain some short-term success. You've got to be careful that you don't do things for the wrong reasons.

A t the end of the season, we have a meeting with each of our players, and I say, "This is my evaluation of the past season and this is how I see your performance." Then we glance ahead and I say, "This is what you've got to do to be better next year."

Always in that conversation, I try to talk with each of the players about his performance as it relates to the team's needs. If a player comes in and says to me, "Coach, what do I have to do to be the best I can be?" and he stops there, then he's not working for the right reason.

The right reason *should* be, "I want to be the best I can be, so the team can be the best it can be." If he stops with "*I* want to be the best *I* can be," then, to me, he is a candidate for the disease of self. In other words, he wants to be the best he can be so that he can be a first-round draft choice or a millionaire basketball player or an All-American.

But if he says, "I want to be the best I can be because my team needs that," then he understands that if the team is good, the other things will take care of themselves. You need to do things for the right reasons.

N obody can win all the time. How you deal with the losses actually becomes more important than the losses themselves. Dealing realistically with losing is the best way to overcome its effects. Understanding that losses are going to come should help you retain your sense of self-worth. If you start looking at yourself and saying, "There are spots on me. There's something wrong with me. What am I doing wrong? I'm trying hard. Why am I losing?" it is self-defeating. Your sense of worth diminishes.

Somehow you've got to get past evaluating yourself solely on the wins and losses because, just as winning gives you an exaggerated self-worth, losing devalues you too much. And in truth, neither is real. Somewhere in between is where you need to place your trust, or establish your worth.

I try to remind myself of that all the time — that we're neither as good as we think we are, nor are we as bad as some may think. We're somewhere in between.

The other thing that I try to remind myself is that nothing is permanent. Even though I have the title of head coach, I'm an interim head coach at Wake Forest. In a sense, I'm interim between Bob Staak, who coached before me, and the coach who will follow me.

So don't try to make things too permanent. The only thing that's permanent is the now, "the precious present," and that's fleeting.

My mother used to say, "All things will pass," and they do. Losing is not something that's going to be with you forever. You've just got to get by it. Just as you don't want to let the wins lead to slippage, you don't want the losses to lead to self-depreciation.

It seems that too often, the farther along the coaching trail you go, the more you have a tendency to separate yourself from the things that really make coaching worthwhile. At this level, you just don't experience things as much as you really want to. For instance, I got a phone call this morning about a kid from Maryland who had come to my basketball camp two years ago. The boy had been in a car accident and was in serious condition.

He's been a big Wake Forest fan all of his life and apparently he had been greatly influenced by our camp—he'd met a lot of our players, and I had said something to him that touched him. One of his dad's friends called and said that one of the things he was asking for was something from the Wake Forest basketball team. When you realize how you've impacted someone's life, especially a young person, it touches you in a very special way.

We live our lives so quickly that we don't realize all the people who are affected by what we do. I don't think they should be, but they are, and that reality should serve as a strong reminder that—as important as basketball is—it is, as my son said, still a game.

# Chapter 9

# A Wife's Perspective

## Lynn A. Odom

*"I feel I've been able to give balance and steadiness to my husband who is in a profession known for its volatility and instability."*

A s a basketball coach's wife, it's probably an understatement to say that basketball structures your life. Your social life revolves around games. Meals are planned with the practice schedule in mind. But at the same time, it's an exciting life, filled with interesting people. And it's never the same; no two years are alike. You watch young players mature and grow up, and before you know it, those freshmen are seniors. The things that sustain me and get me through the season are my faith and the fact that I know David truly loves what he's doing.

D avid and I met at Guilford College and were friends before we began dating. The better we got to know each other, the more I realized he had qualities that were really important to me, like his compassion for other people. He had set definite goals for himself, something a little unusual at his age. He was playing basketball for Guilford, so naturally I began going to the games. I didn't have a strong athletic background—I have two brothers who played high school sports and I enjoyed their games—but I was more interested in activities that weren't athletic in nature.

D avid's wanted to coach ever since I can remember. When he went to my family and told them he wanted to marry me, my Dad asked, "David, what are you going to do?" And he said, "Well, I'm going into coaching." And my Dad said, "But your dad has a successful business. Why would you want to give that up?" But coaching has always been his love.

W hen we got married, I really didn't have any idea about the role of a coach's wife. We were young and not really looking beyond high school coaching. David's first job was in back in his hometown of Goldsboro where he coached almost all sports. I went to all the games, but basketball wasn't central to our lives yet. I'm very close to my family and leaving them and my hometown had been difficult, but it was made so much easier because David's mother, Janie, and sister, Janie Margaret, lived in Goldsboro. Having David's family and friends nearby was wonderful.

A fter four years in Goldsboro we moved to Durham High School. I'll never forget going to Paul and Sarah Williamson's home when Paul interviewed David. At that time, Paul was the head basketball coach and athletic director and was a legend in North Carolina coaching circles.

D avid loved his high school coaching experience. He enjoyed the relationships with the players, and has always told me that he feels that high school coaching is coaching in its purest form.

High school coaches have a sense of security. You don't often read critical things in the newspaper about high school coaches, and seldom is a high school coach fired! Without the pressure of constantly winning and bringing in money, a high school coach can relax and concentrate on developing his players and enjoying the competition.

From my standpoint, I enjoyed the chance to be a part of the high school community. We got to know the players and the other coaches and their families, and occasionally had kids over to our home for a meal. We enjoyed our seven years in Durham, but when the opportunity to move into collegiate sports presented itself, David was ready for the challenge.

W hen David became an assistant coach for Carl Tacy, and we moved from Durham High School to Wake Forest University, one big difference in high school and college coaching became immediately clear: he had been at home a lot more in Durham than he was in Winston-Salem!

In the late seventies, there were no restrictions on when you could recruit. Coaches could travel all the time, and it wasn't unusual for David to be on the road for two or three weeks at a time without coming home. I sometimes hear younger coaches' wives complaining that their husbands seem to be gone all the time and I think, "Boy, if you only knew what it used to be like!"

W hen we moved to Winston-Salem the first time our two boys, Lane and Ryan, were young. Lane was in elementary school and Ryan was around two, and they missed their Dad when he was out of town. However, they've loved being part of his profession. They've gone to ACC tournaments, NCAA tournaments, and the Final Four. They've spent Christmas in Hawaii and traveled to Europe as a result of their dad being a coach. For them to be with their dad and be part of his profession at such an early age was very special.

A fter three years at Wake Forest, David became a Division I head coach when he was named head coach at East Carolina University. I was happily settled in Winston-Salem, close to my family in Greensboro, and the children were involved in their activities, so I can't say I was thrilled to make another move. However, I realized that part of my hesitation was because I'm a little shy, and change is difficult.

But after we got settled in Greenville and met some wonderful friends, we were very happy. The university was the perfect size for us and the team was very good. Winning always makes life better.

As a head coach's wife on the collegiate level for the first time, I felt a need to be at every game and support my husband in every way. I realized for the first time what an asset a supportive coach's wife can be.

A nother three years, and it was time to move again. David and Terry Holland had grown up in eastern North Carolina together, and they had kept track of each other through the years. When approached about an assistant coaching job at the University of Virginia under Terry, David was excited at the opportunity to be coaching in the ACC again.

We loved Charlottesville, and our next-door neighbors, the Hollands. Ann Holland became my coach's wife role model and taught me a lot about handling the stress that comes with being a head coach's wife. Ann is still one of my closest friends; no one understands you like someone who has walked in your shoes!

We lived within walking distance of University Hall and the players felt free to stop by whenever they had a few minutes. And our boys used to ride their bicycles to the coliseum to watch practice.

O ne of the things I learned from Ann was how to deal with the pressure of high expectations. Our first year at Virginia was the year Ralph Sampson was a senior. Virginia was at the top of the polls all season and seemed to be a sure pick for the national championship. When we lost in a heartbreaking defeat to NC State, our hopes were dashed, and the disappointment was incredible. It's difficult not to be overly confident or to get caught up in the excitement, but I've learned that it only takes one loss to end a season, and that it's best to take things one game at a time.

The next year, the pressure was off. Ralph had gone on to his professional career and the Virginia team was not so highly ranked, or so highly pressured. Without those great expectations the team relaxed, had a wonderful season, and we were able to enjoy our delayed trip to the Final Four.

W e spent seven years at Virginia during which David matured as a coach, our children grew up, and I became comfortable being a coach's wife. So when David was selected as head coach and we came to Wake Forest, I felt I was prepared to take on the responsibilities of a head coach's wife. But I was not prepared for the visibility that comes with the job. I'm not very comfortable being in the public eye, and prefer to be a behind-the-scenes person. I don't enjoy giving interviews; I would never want to say anything that could be misconstrued as negative toward David or Wake Forest.

I do enjoy getting to know the players. I don't think of myself as a surrogate mother, although I'm there if they need
me. Tim Duncan stayed with us for a week when he had
chicken pox his freshman year.

Because the players are so busy with classes, and their
schedules vary so much, we have them over to our home in
small groups. We can sit around the table and talk and really
get to know each individual. We had all six freshmen one night
recently and all the upperclassmen the next night. It's always
interesting to see the freshmen adjust and to remember the upperclassmen when they were freshmen. They grow up so fast.

T he hardest thing to deal with as a coach's wife is the intense pain you feel when your husband or a team member
is being criticized. Criticism of a player is the most difficult to
accept, because they are still young and it's tough on them.

On the whole, I think the media has been fair to David.
Unlike David, I do read the newspaper articles about him
and the team, but I don't like reading negative things about a
player. That really bothers me.

O ur first year at Wake Forest was not a great year, and
David got a lot of letters telling him how to coach,
what he should be doing, and who he should be playing. I'm
sure every coach gets those kinds of letters, but when he
brought them home, I would take the comments personally
and would want to write each person back, so he stopped
bringing them home!

I really didn't try to shield the boys from the criticism as
they were growing up. They went to all the games, but
we were somewhat protected because we sat with staff members and family. However, I can remember when Wake Forest

played Kentucky in Charlotte, NC in the NCAAs in 1993 and we played poorly. A fan sitting near us yelled something awful about David. Ryan took offense and went over and confronted the man. They had a heated exchange of words as I was pulling Ryan back to his seat.

I've tried to explain to the boys that fans pay their money to go to the games and that they have the right to express themselves. "I know you want to support your Dad and I understand that, but you are in the public eye and there are some things you must accept without reacting." As they've gotten older, they've learned to control themselves, but sometimes it is hard.

I guess what I want to say to critics is this: A coach doesn't want to lose a ball game. He's not doing something purposely to lose that game. He's working as hard as he can. Maybe he's not doing exactly what the fans or the media think he should be doing, but he knows his team. He has seen them for months in practice and knows what they do best. He knows the chemistry of the team. When you see how many hours my husband puts in, and how tirelessly he works at his job, it's hard to sit by while people criticize him. David has a profound passion for his job, and he's very diligent at it.

The demands on one's time is a problem everyone deals with, and a coach's family is no exception. I try to take care of a lot of things at home so that David is relieved of those kinds of pressures when he does get home. That's not to say that he doesn't help at home; just that he doesn't have much time to help.

Once the season is over, so many people say to me, "What are you and David going to do now that you have some free time?" And I think, "*What* free time?" There are Deacon Club meetings throughout the southeast to attend, and he has speaking engagements scheduled as well as other meetings and commitments that were put off until the end of the season.

D uring the summer, a lot of our time is spent operating basketball camps. For seventeen years, we've operated a Five-Star Women's Camp, which several years ago went from one week each summer to two weeks. At our first camp we had 50 campers; now we have around 200 per week. I handle the administration and planning of the camps. David, Lane, and Ryan hire the coaches and teach during the weeks of the camp. The brochures go out in January, with responses coming in during March and April. It's a busy time through May and June. We all go and stay in the dorms; it has been lots of fun for our family. David runs three weeks of boy's camps at Wake Forest. The people on the Wake Forest basketball staff handle the organization of those camps, so my responsibility isn't as great.

D avid recruits the entire month of July and is gone, so by the middle of August we try to take a week or so for a family vacation. We've realized that in order to get away from David's job it is necessary for us to completely get away from home. As long as we are around, something will come up that "just has to be done." Even something as simple as dinner out with friends has to be done as a spur of the moment thing, because it's hard for us to plan anything relaxing too far in advance.

S eptember is another busy recruiting season, when recruits and their families visit the campus. We go to football

games and entertain them in our home. And then practice begins. Once the season begins, we have many friends and family who come to our games and spend the night with us. It
seems there is always somebody here.

E ven Thanksgiving is taken up by basketball. The players
   stay in town and they practice. Then there is usually a
holiday tournament either right before or right after Christmas, which means the players must cut short the holiday
break so that they can return for practice. When we have in-
ternational players, they stay with us during the holidays,
and those who can't get home also stay here. David may take
a day or two and the players don't get much more than that.
They really do miss those vacations.

If the team is good, it is likely the players will miss spring
break as well. But nobody seems to mind because missing
spring break usually means that you are competing in the
NCAA Tournament, which is every team's goal.

I 've always worried about the time David has had to
  spend away from our family and the impact it has had on
our boys.

Our boys both were active in sports, and David and I
tried to see as many of their games as possible, although I
was able to get to games more often than he was. Since there
is a seven-year age gap between the boys, their games rarely
overlapped, and I went to a lot of games for a number of
years.

During Ryan's senior year (at Hampden-Sydney College)
I went to all of his games, which meant missing quite a few
Wake Forest games. I've also enjoyed watching Lane play (at
High Point University) and coach. It was a special treat when
Wake Forest and the University of Alabama, where he was

an assistant coach, both ended up in Lexington, Kentucky for the first round of the NCAAs in 1994 and we got to see him coach on that level. (Thank goodness we didn't have to play them, because Alabama had beaten Wake Forest twice during the '90–'91 season!)

I always was more anxious watching my children play than watching David coach. They were my children, and they seemed so young and vulnerable.

I don't think I was really surprised when the boys decided to go into their father's profession. But, at the same time, I can't say I encouraged them to become coaches. As children they both played soccer, tennis, and basketball and Lane played a little baseball, too. I encouraged them to play tennis because I love playing tennis and, since they both are David's size, I thought they would be more successful playing tennis than basketball in college.

They probably could have played both, but in college, it's hard to play two sports back-to-back—especially basketball and tennis, because the seasons overlap. They loved tennis, but it required year-round practice. And basketball was their favorite sport from the outset. From there I guess it was a natural progression to go into coaching.

I spend a lot of time keeping everybody, David and the boys, "up." On any given night all three could have games, and it is rare to have three wins. So it is necessary that we all show some compassion for the one who lost. David says that I handle the highs and lows well, that I have balance—but I don't always feel that way!

T here's never a lot of time to either enjoy the wins or an-
guish over the losses — it's always necessary to move on
to the next game. You can beat the number one team in the
country and be on top of the world — and then come home
and be beaten by a lesser team. You've got to recover quickly,
from a loss *or* a win.

R aising a family was always very important to me. That's
not to say that I don't have things that I enjoy other
than my family and my husband's career. I do volunteer work
for organizations that mean a lot to me, serve on several
boards and try to give something back to a community that
has been so good to us. I play tennis and run, both of which
are relaxing and relieve tension. I enjoy spending time with
our family and friends.

I'm going to be co-chair of a fundraiser held in December
benefiting the hospital. Somebody actually said to me, "You
*do* realize that's during the basketball season, and you're
probably going to miss a game or two?!" Yes, I probably will
miss two games, but the reason is compelling and I feel good
about my choice.

S o it's not hard to do other things if you want to. If I had a
full-time career it would be more difficult. I think if you
had an outside career, you would need an awful lot of help. I
would never see David if I didn't participate and go to the
games or if I wasn't able to be here when he got home, just to
talk and be together.

W omen who have spent time preparing for a career
want to be able to practice that profession — and
that's fine. But I think the couple must be willing to compro-

mise to make the marriage work. Any two-career marriage has its conflicts, but if one of the careers is coaching, it becomes doubly difficult. It would be awfully hard because of the demands of the profession itself.

A s a young coach, you have to accept the possibility of moving a lot, especially when you are starting off. That can be hard for a wife with her own profession.

Now, young people are getting married later in life. Their careers are more established before they get married, and they seem to have their lives all planned. David and I were married right out of college. That was just the way it was. You didn't wait until it was "just the right time." I hope both my boys will find somebody who understands about the coaching profession.

I f David loses a game, he is very quiet. I never question him about game situations. I've learned to respect his feelings and to give him a little space after a hard loss. If we have guests at home after a game, and we lose, David is wonderful about putting his need to be alone aside until later.

H aving Tim Duncan play for Wake Forest really brought a lot of attention to David, and when Tim decided to return for his senior year, people tried to give some of the credit to David. While he did offer advice and encouragement, the decision was Tim's to make. But as a result, David was so overwhelmed by requests for his time—for interviews, for speaking engagements, for appearances with the team—that it became quite a distraction.

I think he felt that all the attention focused on Tim distracted the team, and that the expectations for the team made them a little too sure of themselves. But I felt that some of his frustration was that David didn't feel that he was able to concentrate solely on his team, because the outside things were so demanding.

L ooking back, I can't imagine a more exciting life than the one David and I have had together. It hasn't been without its challenges, but no marriage is without challenges. It has given us the opportunity to live in different places, to meet many wonderful people, and to watch young people grow and mature and be better people for having played on my husband's teams. It has taught me self-reliance and independence, but I've been able to give balance and steadiness to my husband who is in a profession known for its volatility and instability.

# Chapter 10

# "Guardians of the Game"

*"No geniuses in the game?"*

S omeone said that the will to win is not nearly as important as the will to prepare to win. I think you teach kids
that by concentrating on the present, by trying to improve
today. You keep constantly hammering that they can't worry
about next week or next month until they arrive.

Let's concern ourselves with today. If we can do that,
then the preparation will take care of itself. It will be a daily
process. The hardest thing is that everyone wants to see results *now*.

B uilding a basketball program or a basketball team is like
building a house. You may not notice a difference over a
few days or even over a week or two, but you know that the
builders have been working on it every day, so you know
changes have been made. In basketball, you do certain things
daily and you don't notice them having a big effect on you,
but over the course of time, one day affects the next. It gives
you a stronger foundation. You put one brick on top of the
other and you grow.

You have to continue to remind yourself that you are improving and acknowledge that preparation is taking place,

even though you're not saying, "Let's prepare to win." Being prepared is the culmination of all the work; it's the coming together of the work that you do every day.

T he older you get, the more you realize that building a program, building something that's solid, takes time. It's not going to be done in one day. I have a bit more patience now, and that's what we're talking about—patience. Recognizing that patience is necessary for something solid to be established is tough for young coaches.

Patience is a tremendous virtue, particularly when working with young people. Just as every kid grows physically at his or her own pace, so, too, do young adults develop at their own rates mentally and psychologically. The process of maturation can take its toll on anyone. Patience and hard work seem to help the most.

A dministering a sports program entails a number of skills beyond those on the court or the field. A certain amount of formal training is needed, but a lot of it you learn in a practical manner, like living. As private citizens, my wife and I have a bank account and we've learned to balance it. We know how much is coming in and how much is going out, and hopefully there's a plus sign at the end of the month.

You develop these skills as you go along. It's easy to spend somebody else's money. Even high school coaches have budgets, and it's important that they stay within those budgets. It's also important to understand that nobody has as much money as they want or think they need. There's a challenge in that—you try to do with less so that others will have more. There's a lesson there.

In coaching today, you've got what I call the "'90s coach"— a coach who has gone to school to learn how to be a coach. They are more programmed. They are more computerized. They are more into technique. I think, however, they run the risk of over-coaching their teams and their players.

Then there are the opposites. There are those of us who coach by the seat of our pants, with fire in our bellies—and probably neither extreme is totally right. You need to have a middle ground in there someplace.

Those of us who coach by the seat of our pants probably aren't as organized as we need to be, at least outwardly. If a weed appears in my garden, I deal with it quickly by applying weed killer. In coaching our teams, we should follow the same process. At the first sign of something going awry, we should attack it and correct it.

Those who are programmed have a tendency to out-think themselves. They look at things and say, "Well, let's see what the numbers say. Let's go back and get the percentages on what's going to happen if we foul our opponent's star player at the end of the game, and let's see what his percentage is in the last three minutes. We know he shoots 74% for his career, but what does he shoot in the last 38 seconds of the game?"

At some point it's your head or your heart. You just *know* that this is what you should be doing and you find a way to get it done. I'm not a '90s coach, although there may be some advantages to being one.

I've seen coaching change to the point where the younger coaches rely on the Internet. They coach by computer, by statistics, by film. Basketball is a game—a game played by humans—and the human element will always be present and should be appreciated.

In strategy sessions, one coach sets up a play on the board. Another coach puts a defense up to stop it. Then the first coach comes back with the reply, "Yeah, but I've got a great counter to your defense. He beats the defense because he had the pen in his hand last.

The game's not played that way. People lose sight of the human element. Things change. You've got to be flexible. You've got to be adaptable.

T he new breed of coaches is more into influencing the game through structure. I don't think that's a product just of youth, but of the times. I didn't feel that way as a young coach. We had structure and we had discipline, but it didn't come from a sheet of paper. I think I'm a better coach now because I have the ability to supply emotion on days when it's needed, yet I have the ability to let the players play when they can supply their own emotion. I can back away and let things happen.

A t one point I felt as if I had to be involved in everything, and if I wasn't, then I would not be doing my job. I felt somewhat inadequate. At some point you need to relax and let your players play the game. Things are going to happen — you just need to know *when* to let them happen. Guide things along, and they will usually work out right.

Y ou've got to be able to adjust. That's what life is — a series of adjustments. Coaching is very much like that. You go into each game or into each practice with a plan but, because you are dealing with a human element, you have to adjust in midstream. The best coaches are those who are able to do that; they're the ones who are able to put a plan together, yet understand and prepare their players for change.

Young coaches today are very capable from a technical standpoint. They have great knowledge. What they've got to learn is the other side of it—how to take all the knowledge that they have and translate it into "people" terms. They need to learn how to get their players to complement each other. They need to have five men playing as one.

Every coach has been faced with losing his or her temper. Sometimes it's all right to lose your temper, but *when* you lose it is important, and *where* you lose it is important.

If you've got a temper, you need to exorcise it, or you need to learn to deal with it. It's very hard, because things happen at the most inopportune times. It's important that you keep a handle on it. If you've got a temper, you need to have an outlet for it because if you don't, it's going to explode sooner or later—and you don't want it to come out at the wrong time. The more crucial the situation, the greater the need to exercise control.

One reason I like basketball over other sports is because basketball is a game of spontaneous decision making. It is a game played in motion all of the time. As you go up the court, there are no guarantees where people are going to be.

You're playing not only against your opponent; you're playing against the clock, you're playing against the environment, you're playing against yourself. Your ability—or your inability—to make something happen with all these forces working against you, speaks directly to your degree of preparation and your ability to channel your emotions.

One of the things I've learned over the years is respect for the opposition. No matter what you do or how good you are, everything happens in relation to who you are playing and what the stakes are. The other team has a lot to say about how good you are going to be on any given night.

Sometimes coaches will say, "We don't worry about who we're playing, we're just going to do what we do." There may be some validity in that, but you still must acknowledge that the other team affects how you perform. As good as Tim Duncan was, he could be stopped. If you put a guy in front of him and a guy behind him and he isn't able to touch the basketball the whole game, there's only so much he can do.

A s a leader, you shouldn't ask anyone to do something you wouldn't do yourself or that you haven't done yourself. You don't want to be too outrageous in your demands. You want to make sure that you are realistic in what you ask of others—both your staff and your players.

S omeone said, "Leaders without followers are impotent. Leaders with talentless followers are ineffective." A good leader is one who knows when it's his or her time, and is not afraid of the final results of his leadership. He's not afraid of taking the lead. In taking the lead, he understands that things may not turn out the way he or others want them to, but he's not afraid of the end result.

A good leader is also a person who knows when it's time to delegate to others and let them take the lead. That's one of the traps that young coaches fall into—I know I did. When you've just become a head coach, you have a tendency to want to have your fingerprint on everything that's done. And in so doing, you spread yourself too thin and you do a little bit of everything, but nothing well.

Many things get left undone when you try to do every-thing yourself. When you have capable people around you, give them a job and then let them do it.

I recommend combining one's practical knowledge of a sport with formal training. The coaching classes I had in college were very valuable, because the football coach taught about how to coach football and the basketball coach taught about coaching basketball. But the best way for me to learn was to combine that formal learning with the practical side of "living the life." I studied as hard outside the classroom as I did inside the classroom.

In basketball, my size obviously dictated that I played guard. But I spent as much time listening to my college coach teach big man play as I did listening to him coach me. I knew if I was going to coach basketball, eventually I was going get a Tim Duncan or a Ralph Sampson, and I was going to have to know how to teach them.

My size encourages tall players like Ralph Sampson or Tim Duncan to ask, "What do you know about big man play? You're not big!" So I have to counter that by proving that I know as much about post play as I do about coaching guards. I spent a lot of time outside the classroom learning those things that were not natural for me.

Football is the same way. If you're going to coach, no matter what position you played, you have to know how to teach a right guard and a right tackle to work as one. I was a quarterback, but I had to know what everybody on the team did on every play. I could make a call in the huddle, we'd start to the line, and the left tackle would ask, "Who do I block?" I had to know exactly who he was supposed to block so I could say, "Block down" or "Double team" or "Pull and go." I always made a point of knowing. I had to know.

We say good players can play in the present and great players can play in the future. The same is true for coaches. The great ones coach "the now" very well, but they coach even better two or three plays ahead. I think the ability to do that is innate; it can only be learned to a certain extent.

Instinctively, we do what we're good at, and that's not peculiar only to athletics or to coaching. A person who crunches numbers all day long in a computer lab does that because he or she is good at it. But at some point you have to find enjoyment in what you do as well. There has to be a fulfillment in seeing it all come together. The best players and the best coaches are those who have the innate ability to perceive what sport's all about.

It's been the general consensus that great players don't make great coaches. I don't think that's necessarily true. Larry Bird's trying to prove that premise wrong now. We'll see what happens. He may not have the patience to be a good coach. Let's hope he does.

The problem that great players have in becoming great coaches—and this is something that can be overcome—is that generally, the great players who are the Stradivarii of their professions—people like Magic Johnson, Michael Jordan, Larry Bird, Babe Ruth, Ty Cobb, Mickey Mantle, Johnny Unitas, or John Elway—were incredibly gifted athletes. They demanded a great deal of themselves, but so much of what they accomplished individually was so easy for them that they couldn't understand or appreciate the struggles of those who were less talented.

"What do you mean you can't jump up and dunk it any time you want to?" "What's so hard about hitting a curve ball?" Or, "Why can't you read that defense if you're a quarterback? What's so hard about that?"

Great athletes often don't understand the imperfections of the less-talented athlete and they have a tendency to be impatient where patience is needed. If they could overcome that sense of impatience, if they could somehow bring themselves down in their thinking so that they could relate to the less-talented athlete, then their chances of being great coaches would be enhanced.

A thletes who have been great players—truly great players—are people whose mentality is to control a situation. Michael Jordan controls the end of the game: "I'm going to take the shot." As a coach you can't always do that. We all become control freaks to a certain extent.

Trusting others becomes the central issue. You don't want to admit that you don't trust your teammates or you don't trust your players, but you know what's right and you know how it should be done, and you have a tendency to want to do it yourself.

As a coach you can't do that. You have to hand the baton over and show great faith and confidence in your players. That's hard for people who have been the ones who have been doing it. They've been swinging the bat or making the toss or shooting the shot that decides the game, and it's hard for them to relinquish that control. That's a trait that they have to learn, and because it's hard for them, they really have to work at it.

B eing a great player doesn't necessarily give you the administrative skills or the people skills necessary to be a
good coach. As a player, you don't think as a coach. You
think for yourself, but not for everybody else; or your talent is so instinctive that you don't really think, you just
"do."

U sually I'm more comfortable knowing what's about to
happen. That doesn't mean that if things don't go as
planned, I'm going to be uncomfortable. I know if I go into a
game and things don't happen the way that I want, I can adjust. But I still want a plan in my own mind. I have to visualize what's about to happen.

The same is true in working with my team. If I can't visualize a certain play or a certain tactic working, then it's hard
for me to believe that my team could visualize it, much less
perform it. So I talk with them. I want them comfortable.

I don't look at coaching as a corporate job. Whenever I
ask my team to do something or to make some sacrifice, I feel
that my staff and I have to be willing to make the same sacrifice—within the context that we're coaches and they're players. It's the same whether they are working for us on the basketball floor or we're supporting them in one of their other
endeavors, like academics.

L oyalty in the face of adversity is a powerful ingredient
for coaching. You have to be loyal to yourself, your values, and your morals. You are loyal to your staff and you are
loyal to your players and to your university. Sometimes you
make decisions which in the short term may not be in the
team's best interest, but you know that in the long term, the
decisions you made will be beneficial.

S etting goals can get in the way of understanding and appreciating the present. I don't do a lot of goal setting. I have a few goals which are the same every year, mostly short-term goals. They are: Have a winning season. If you have a winning season, you had a great year. I also want to be a positive factor in the conference race as it winds down. I want to try to win the conference championship and the tournament and then go as far as we can in the NCAA Tournament. If we get deep into the tournament, I want to try to win the national championship—but I don't worry about that early on.

E very year I try to attack each of the goals as we go along. When we get to the point where, mathematically, we have secured a winning season, I make a big deal out of it. I know how many games we've got scheduled, and I know when a winning season is assured.

I say, "Aha! You know what tonight is? You just guaranteed yourselves a winning season!" That's big to me.

T here's a saying, "The two greatest things you can give your children are roots and wings." I think that's also what you want to do with both your players and your assistant coaches. If you are loyal to a person, in a sense you love them. And when you love them, you want what's best for them, even if what's best for them is not always what's best for you. It may be hard to do, but you know it's right and you make your decisions accordingly. At some point, you come to grips with it. Nothing stays the same. It either gets better or it gets worse, but it changes.

O ne of the greatest mistakes you can make is trying to keep things the same. They shouldn't be the same, and to try and keep them that way is wrong. That's why it's hard to go back in time. To feel, "I wish everything was the same as it was in 1972" is wrong; you can't do that. You can't go back in time or in relationships.

It's similar to having a long relationship with a girl. If you break up and are apart for some period of time and then try to get back together, it's very difficult. You lose something. I never faced that because all the way through college I always had one girl, but I saw others trying to do it. Some people go back to their high school reunions and want to go back in time. Rarely can you do that.

I t has been asked whether players more often make good plays to win games, or are more likely to make mistakes that lose games. I think more games are lost because of mistakes made, than games won by great shots.

Most of the time, field goal percentages are in the forties. That's less than half. You've missed more than you made. But that's not necessarily bad, because everything is relative.

There is a certain value in just hanging in there. Maybe you're not doing a lot to win the game, but you're giving the others a chance to lose it, and generally they will. You just hang onto the ball for one more pass or five more seconds. Through the course of the game, that puts you in control.

I 've been asked whether I'd rather score 100 points and win, or hold the other team to 36 and win. Ideally you would like to do both. I don't go into games saying that we've got to score 70 or 80 points to win, or that we've got to hold them to 50 points or less, because as the game unfolds, it's invariably different than you planned. Good teams can adjust to any situation.

I never go into a game saying that we should win by 25 points. I do go into some games knowing that we're the better team, and that if we play our best and they play their best, we're going to win the basketball game. That's always my goal — to have our team playing our best. Then the final score becomes secondary.

I don't try to predetermine the outcome of a game. I do try to visualize how we can win a game, but I don't concern myself with how we might beat the other team by 20 points.

I don't really have a pre-game ritual; maybe it's more like a pre-game routine. I don't wear certain colors when we're playing or a certain pair of underwear or red socks or anything like that. I try not to relate specific clothes to winning or losing, because then you tend to lose sight of the important aspects of game preparation. However, there are certain things I do on a game day that make me feel comfortable. For instance, I like time by myself to prepare mentally and emotionally for what's likely to be a volatile night. People may try to turn routines into rituals and then into superstitions. I try not to do that.

I try not to get my players "up" for a game. I want them to be up every day. Every year, I begin with the understanding that you play hard every single possession, which means you play hard every single practice, which means you play hard every single game.

If you do that, you don't have to worry about the emotional tone of a game. I prefer more of a business-like approach to the games. I look at it as, "This is a game in which we have the opportunity to improve. If we do that, I'll be happy." I try not to manufacture false emotion. Emotion will only take you so far, because you can use up all of your emotional energy, only to fall short at the end. In the end, your depth of preparation and your ability to execute under pressure should be enough.

T he game of basketball hasn't changed that much during my coaching career. There have been some rule changes —the 35-second clock, the 5-second count, the 3-point line. Those are really cosmetic changes, though they have changed the game some.

Basically, the game is still a game played in motion in a spontaneous manner. If you over-coach it, you take away the spontaneity and the beauty of basketball.

I'm guilty just like others of over-coaching at times. I try not to, and the best teams that I've been associated with or had a chance to coach were teams that were spontaneously great. They just "had it"—and how you teach that I'm not sure. We'd do it every year if we could, because the best teams are those that play together with heart.

Y ou take something from every coach you work for, just as I did from every coach that I played for. In the late '70s, when I was an assistant at Wake Forest, Carl Tacy taught me that you will be what you practice every day. He was an offensive coach who loved the jump shot. He was a fast-break coach and I have yet to be around anyone who taught that style better. That's how he wanted his teams to play, and that's what we practiced.

His teams were very good passers and very good shooters, and they played quickly. Ideally, you play like you practice. Carl Tacy's teams proved that beyond any doubt.

T erry Holland at Virginia was an excellent technical coach who taught me that there's always another way.

He and I used to get into philosophical discussions about how to attack a defense or how to defend another team. While some people are very structured and cling to one point of view, Terry had the ability to look at things from different angles and say, "Yeah, this is right, but let's also think about doing it a different way." That approach has great validity. It's such an advantage to be able to look at things through different lenses, in different ways, and from different points of view.

There are different philosophies as to when a coach should abandon his or her game plan. One is, that you never abandon it. You never give up on it. If you practiced something and you taught it correctly, it will eventually work if you stay with it long enough.

Basically that's true, but at some point you may feel the anxiety and frustration of your team. If you're the one who feels frustrated, that's probably not the time to change. You need to show more confidence in yourself and in your plan. But when you begin to feel you're losing your team and you need to get their attention again, it may be time to look at something different.

It comes back to the system itself. If your system is solid, your players know who you are by what you teach. They know what you teach by who you are. For instance, if you're a confirmed man-to-man coach and you suggest, in the most important game of the year, that your team play zone, most players will question your confidence in them and in the style of play that has gotten you to that point. You don't want to do that sort of thing. Remember, confidence is hard to build, yet easy to lose.

Y ou've got to be careful about changing in midstream. That said, I think one of the best coaching jobs in our league in 1997 was done by Mike Krzyzewski, who did change in midstream. Right in the middle of the year he changed the way he was coaching and the way his team played.

He's never told me this, but I think he looked at Wake Forest and thought, "In order to beat Wake Forest we need change—change in our lineup and change in our style." So he found a reason to get Greg Newton out of the line-up and went 180 degrees in the other direction. He went from being a fairly big team with Newton and Taymon Domzalski, both 6'10" or better, to being one of the smallest teams in memory. I think he made the decision at the time, saying, "This lineup we've got—this big lineup—is not going to take us very far. A smaller lineup gives us a better chance." And it did. He made the right decision.

T he older I've gotten, the more I've tried to get away from measuring myself or my teams by won/lost records or championships won or lost. I've focused more on the experience, the enjoyment of the experience, the day-to-day challenge of trying to get better. You want to ask yourself, "What can we do today to make ourselves better?"

If you focus on that and don't have a tendency to glance too far in the future, then you've got a better chance of shouldering the responsibilities of the present. That's doable, that's possible.

For me to worry about what's going to happen on April 1 when it's only November 1 is crazy. You can only do that in terms of long-range planning. You can't play a championship game in November when, in fact, the game is not scheduled until March or April. If you play a championship game in your mind every day, it becomes too much of a burden.

I heard a coach say one time that there are no geniuses in this game. I don't know if that's completely accurate, but probably so. As "guardians of the game," all of us—genius or not—are obligated to share with each other.

# Chapter 11

# It's Just a Game

*"When the ball goes up on Saturday afternoon,
everybody's even."*

Young people today confuse what they do best, with
what they enjoy, and the desire to make a lot of money.
All three areas are important, but can conflict with each
other. In the end, if you don't choose the thing you enjoy
most, you run the risk of being dissatisfied or unsuccessful,
and then having to regroup and start again.

At the end of our '96–'97 season, things started changing
in Tim Duncan's life. He was being offered opportunities that most people only dream about. Since Tim wasn't
fielding a lot of phone calls or inquiries, most of them came
across my desk. I didn't even bother him with most of them,
because I knew he wouldn't be interested, but one particular
call seemed different.

A businessman from the Dallas, Texas area called me and
said, "Coach, I want to make a proposition for Tim Duncan." I said, "What's it like?"

And he said, "Well, I own 12 stores in the Dallas area
and they are spread out throughout the whole metroplex. I

will send a private plane to pick up Tim on a Thursday and get him oriented to the area Friday."

"Then, on Saturday, I want to take him around from store to store and let him sign some autographs and answer some questions. We'll have a big press conference and it'll be great PR for my stores. I'll have him home on Saturday night." And I asked, "What does Tim get in return?"

He said, "I'll pay him $50,000 for his day's work." I said, "That's a considerable amount of money. I certainly feel compelled to ask Tim about that. How about putting that on paper and faxing it to me? I'll give it to him and let him consider it and I'll get back in touch with you." So he faxed all the information, including the date and the times that he wanted Tim to appear.

The next day I told Tim about my conversation and said, "Timmy, this is one you might want to look at." He hadn't shown any interest at all in doing that type of thing, but I thought considering the amount of money, I shouldn't make the decision for him. He needed to be the one to make it.

Tim read it and looked at me and said, "Coach, I'd appreciate it if you would call the guy and tell him I'm not interested."

I said, "Timmy, did you see the amount of money offered? That's $50,000 for one day. I know in a couple of months you're likely to have all the money you need, but this would serve as a pretty good bridge for the next two or three months until you get your first NBA check."

And he said, "Coach, I really appreciate that, but I'm not going anywhere on that day." I asked, "Why?" And he said, "April 25 is my birthday and I'm not going to spend my birthday with people I don't know, in a place I've never been. I want to be here in Winston-Salem at Wake Forest with my friends."

That speaks volumes about the kind of person that he is. He wouldn't trade his own private time even for $50,000. Clearly, Tim understood the difference between financial gain and personal satisfaction.

K ids coming along today are products of their environments. I am a product of a different era. To me, you do what comes naturally to you, you don't confuse yourself, and you don't let others confuse you. Today, so much is being thrown at kids that things become confusing to them.

S till, I have a hard time understanding people who say they can't make up their minds as to what they want to do. They don't want to commit. They want to stay in a gray area so that they retain all the choices. To me, it's easy. You just ask yourself, "Do I want to be a banker?" "Do I want to be in marketing?" "Do I want to be a teacher?" Ask yourself, "What do you do best? Where do you find enjoyment?"

W ork quickly to find your level of comfort and where you are best suited to be. Not everyone's suited to be an NBA Coach. Not everyone's suited to be a youth coach. Find your level and be satisfied with it, be happy with it. Don't be somebody who always wants to be somebody else.

I don't think there's much career-switching by coaches. Now, you play the game from the bench and get paid for it. You are still part of the sport and you are touching lives.

S ome of the greatest accomplishments that I've ever witnessed came about because the people involved gave up their personal desires for the good of the group or the good of the cause. Then the group becomes one; it is unified. Coaching in its purest sense is getting the group or the team to play as one.

A key ingredient for any coach is loyalty, because it is such a volatile profession and, at times, it becomes too competitive. Everybody wants what somebody else has, whether it's his job or his knowledge, his championship or his money. It can be unforgiving at times.

T he ball is the greatest unifier, yet the greatest divider. Only family and religion can unify (or divide) as much as sport. You can't find another profession with a greater common denominator, or one which unifies the masses (players, coaches, alumni, fans) as much.

A university has a lot of constituents, yet when it comes time for a basketball team to play, there are no divisions. Everyone wants the same thing. They may want it in different ways, but they want us to win. Some people may say, "I wish he would press more" or "I wish he'd run more." But when it's all said and done, they don't care. The end result is, "Coach, don't embarrass me."

As people begin work Monday morning over coffee at the local brokerage firm, or in a lawyer's office, or at a bank, I guarantee they're not talking about the stock market. They're talking about the games over the weekend. Sports are entertainment, but they are also a tremendous unifier. A week ends with games being played, and they are a point of departure for the next week.

S ome people argue that student athletes should be paid, that they're virtually professional athletes, but I disagree. Clearly, they are rewarded for what they do, but it is an educational grant and I don't look at it as being professional in nature. It's more of an exchange—in exchange for your participation on the athletic front, we will provide you with a scholarship to study and learn.

T he NCAA rules are changing as to whether an athlete can work during the school year, but at a place like Wake Forest, it would be very hard. There's been talk of providing scholarship players with a certain stipend each month for their personal needs, and I think that's okay. I know it's tough for students who come from less advantaged situations to sustain themselves in college without help.

B ut let's not forget that they don't have to go to college. College isn't mandatory. You choose to go to college or to go to work. If you choose the latter, you can work until you get enough money to go and be like everybody else.

People shouldn't blame the system; the system doesn't put kids in college. It's a non-compulsory system. You choose to go to college because you know it will be to your benefit.

T he NCAA has done a pretty good job of making it possible for disadvantaged student-athletes to get assistance. With Pell Grants, a needy student can get as much as $2,700 a year through the federal government if he or she qualifies.

Each year, more than one student refuses to fill out those forms because they are embarrassed. All they've got to do is fill them out and send them into the federal government and they'll get $1,350 a semester. That's pretty good money.

There's also a special assistance fund provided by the NCAA and administered by the ACC office. A student-athlete can go to our compliance office and receive as much as $500 per year. For instance, in the winter, a student might need a coat and a sweater, or they might have to make an emergency flight home. All the student-athlete has to do is apply and, once approved, get a check, go buy whatever is needed, and take the receipt back as proof of purchase. That's the end of it. They don't have to pay it back. It's interesting, though, that at a recent conference meeting it was reported that not a single school had used all of their emergency fund money.

W hen you view these things from the inside, situations are not always as the public perceives them to be. I've had kids tell me, "I'm not going to fill that thing out. I'm not going to send it home." When you hear that, you might have difficulty understanding or appreciating the real need that some of these athletes might have. Their need causes them to feel different and they don't want to do anything that might exacerbate the situation.

What do you do about it? The very student-athletes who may financially need jobs are often the kids who need extra academic help. How are they going to find the time for both?

The new NCAA rule suggests that a student-athlete can work and earn up to the difference between the cost of a scholarship and the cost of attendance. A scholarship covers room, board, tuition, books, and supplies. The cost of attendance includes what it costs to go to school above those things—money for haircuts, laundry, eating out, or clothes. The figure varies from school to school, but the difference can be as much as $3,500 a year.

In order to work, a student would have to sacrifice something, and you know it's not going to be basketball. It's more likely to be their studies.

F ar and away the majority of the athletes who spend any time in college leave better than when they entered. Whether they graduate or not, they're better for the experience. If a kid leaves early to go to the NBA, he's still better for the experience. The kid who goes four years to college and doesn't graduate, but plays basketball or football, is better for the experience.

Being an athlete gives students a jump start on life because of the discipline required and the motivation they feel to succeed. Sports teaches young people passion and teaches them to deal with pressure and make decisions. Student-athletes get everything that regular students get, plus another experience that's extraordinary and guaranteed to help them in life.

F ans often live their lives vicariously through sports and their favorite athlete. There are a lot of armchair quarterbacks and armchair coaches who, on Sunday afternoons watching an NFL game, live their lives through Troy Aikman, Brett Favre, or Bill Parcells. There are probably people who live their lives vicariously through me.

There are frustrated athletes who think to themselves, "I could have been Michael Jordan, but I didn't get the opportunities that he got." But there are other fans who follow sports because it gives them identification. The lines of allegiance are well-defined and, when their team is winning, the fans have a sense of self-esteem, because that's who they are. "I wear the black and gold." "I wear the blue and white." "I'm a Hornet." "I'm a Panther." Sports get people away from the wear and tear and routine of their daily lives.

P layed at the very highest level, sports can be perceived as purely entertainment. Everyone is fighting for the entertainment dollar. The public makes heroes or heels out of sport celebrities.

S ports can also be an outlet, a recreational outlet. It's psy-chologically liberating to go to a basketball game on a Saturday afternoon and scream your lungs out. It can be good therapy.

You can let out a great deal of the frustration and anxi-eties that you built up during the course of watching the stock market go up and down, or swinging a sledge hammer, or laying brick, or whatever you happen to do.

W hen the ball goes up on Saturday afternoon, every-body's even. It makes no difference whether you're a millionaire or a factory worker, you're all the same. Sports have a way of bringing everybody back to the starting point. For two hours, you're all together. It's great.

Edwin Cady, an emeritus professor of English at Duke University and a former faculty representative to the NCAA, once raised the question, "Where, indeed, can you see and hear a hard hat who never finished high school and a scien-tist with three degrees stand side by side and sing the foolish and vulgar tune of 'Alma Mater' with a fervor and unction fit for a Bach chorale sung by believers." (*Greensboro Daily News*, Nov. 12, 1978, quoted in Herb Appenzeller, *Sports and the Courts*.)

S elf-discipline and time management are two vitally im-portant aspects of successful people's lives and are among the first things that we try to teach our freshmen when they arrive. You teach them in subtle ways every day, because those are tough things for kids to grasp.

Typically, high school students have their time managed for them. They go to school at 8:00 a.m. and get out at 3:00 p.m., and every minute of their seven-hour day is planned for them.

They get to college and they've got three hours of class and four hours of "What do I do?" Their choices range anywhere from "see my girlfriend," to "go to the library," to "do more lab work," to "sleep"—and, as their mentor, you've got to help them prioritize.

I find my own window of opportunity out running by myself. Talking to myself as I run, I do some of my best work. People might argue that that's not getting away, but it is for me. It's away from the phone. It's away from questions. It's away from conversation.

Kids are starting more serious sports competition at an earlier age and I'm not sure that's good. I *do* think sport is good at an early age, but it should be less structured and more free play—no trophies, no worry about championships. Play for fun, for exercise, for good health. That's what I'd like to see young people doing.

Specialization by youngsters is forced too early. My experience as a high school coach was that my best teams were teams that had kids who played three sports—football, basketball, and baseball. The players were able to take the experience of playing one sport and transfer it to another. In a sense, the skills are interchangeable.

I don't like to see early specialization unless it's a youngster who has extraordinary skills, like a Tiger Woods. Maybe you don't want to mess with nature there. When nature has given one person such exceptional skills and abilities, then it's probably right to go ahead and develop them. Still, everybody needs balance.

M aybe we want our kids to start growing up too soon. What makes five the right age to start school? Maybe six or seven is just as good. Maybe we should let kids be a little more psychologically and emotionally prepared before they start off to school.

The same thing is true athletically. Who says a swimmer has to be swimming seriously by age 13 or he or she is not going to make it? Maybe 15 is okay. Swimmers start so young that they are almost considered past their prime once they pass the age of 20. Maybe that's not really right. Maybe that's just the way we see things right now. Could it be that having a youngster specialize at such an early age is a phenomenon created by selfish coaches?

A s we've gotten into the late '90s, we have certain tracks that we put athletes on and we say, "This track is your best chance to be successful at the very highest level."

I'm not sure that is totally true or that it should be totally true. You've got to let everybody develop in their own way. Tim Duncan is a great example of someone who didn't do the classic things to help himself as a youngster. There are ways to catch up if you don't get a great jump-start. As a matter of fact, there's some value to coming in almost unmolded and being able to shape yourself later in life.

I know this from my own experience, because as an undergraduate, although I never had any doubt that I was going to graduate, I wasn't a really great student. Yet I found learning to be a lot easier once I got to the graduate level. I don't know whether that was because I was paying for it myself (instead of my parents) or whether it was just easier for me because I was mature enough to appreciate the experience.

O ur basketball camp numbers at Wake Forest have really grown over the years and there are probably several reasons—identification with a winning team, love of the game, and wanting to go to camp where Tim Duncan played. A lot of parents send their kids to camp here because they want them exposed to their university, their alma mater. There's also a certain segment of our population that wants their kids occupied for a week so they can go to the Caribbean on vacation.

Then there are parents who really want their kids exposed to basketball. Hopefully, the way we've run our camps over the last eight years makes them feel that we do a good job teaching and caring for their children. Of course, some kids come mainly for the social aspects of camp.

Camps emphasizing individual sports are a product of the '80s. When I was growing up, camping was living out of doors and learning how to build a fire. Putting sticks together—that was camping. This is not camp. It's camp, but it's not camp in the pure sense of the word.

T itle IX has had a big effect on sports. It's something we needed to come to grips with—which again goes back to the idea of doing things for the right reasons. Certainly no one can argue that if the purpose of Title IX is opportunity where opportunity has been denied, then it's good. Although it forces some painful things to occur, I think Title IX is well-intentioned. But some of the results are almost inexplicable.

Making the necessary changes is like building roads in areas of rapid population growth. In some cities, you can't build the roads fast enough to take care of the growing number of cars. Title IX is that way. You can't even up, in a few short years, all of the inequities that have existed for decades. Some people are having a problem determining whether progress is being made or not. In effect, and in fact, we *are* making a lot of progress.

The people pushing Title IX and gender equity don't want to acknowledge too many gains, because they feel there is still much work to be done. But while they may not acknowledge things, they've got to be fairly pleased with the progress that women have made in sports.

In the short term, women's gains may mean losses for the men, but I think we'll get it back. Men's basketball is one of the areas that has been impacted the most. In basketball, women now have 15 scholarships and men have 13. Two scholarships have been taken away from us. That doesn't seem right when the two teams are the same size, but it's not a question of basketball versus basketball. Title IX looks at the percentage of women and men in a student body and the percentage of sports opportunities for each gender.

Football is the problem when you get right down to it, because there's no equal for football on the women's side and football teams are so large. What men are saying is, "Look, take football out of the equation." Women are saying, "You can't take football out."

The number of scholarships should be sport-specific. Men's and women's basketball should have the same number of scholarships. Men's baseball and women's softball should have the same number. Any sport that requires the same number of players should have the same number of opportunities.

Y ou'll see more and more women coaching men's sports in the future. There are some female assistant coaches for men's college teams now, and you see it more often at the high school level. For instance, at Hoggard High School in Wilmington, North Carolina, the head boy's coach is currently a woman. Of course, you often see men coaching women's teams, but I think the reverse will start being more common. The 1997 hiring of two women as full-time referees in the NBA is another positive sign of how things are changing.

A ny coach who says that his team hasn't surprised him somewhere along the way isn't telling the truth. Surprise can be good. If a coach could predict everything that was going to happen before the fact, it would take away the essence of the game. You want the spontaneity—that's the nature of the game.

T he teams that I have enjoyed the most were those that were content with themselves, those that did the best that they could do, and those that were teams of individuals who gave more than they received. They gave to each other. They gave of themselves, and they appreciated each other.

T he worst feeling in the world is not living up to yourself—not doing what you know you should do, or have the ability to do, because you didn't give the amount of effort needed to do it. Do I care enough to give my very best? Am I disciplined enough to do it every day?

W e're not all given Michael Jordan's talent, but we all have the ability to do our best every day. When you do less than that, it becomes unacceptable.

T here are certainly different ways to define success, but the bottom line is that you compete against yourself, against your own potential, against your own abilities. Everyone has different abilities, but the question really is, "How close do *I* come to maximizing *my* potential?" When you do that, I think you've got to let it rest.

# Chapter 12

# When the
# Whistle Blows

*"There are very few secrets in the game."*

At the college level, there is so much talent, and teams know so much about each other, that there are very few surprises. We're around each other all the time and we see almost every game on television. If anything, we're overexposed to each other.

At the high school level, you know less about your opponents because you just don't see each other as much. Perhaps, in this case, less is better, because basically the game is not that complicated. You've got an offense and a defense, and how you attack and how you get your players to execute is basically the same.

The magic of this sport is found in questions such as, "Why does a certain team continue to play well on the road when others can't?" That's an interesting phenomenon to me. Maybe it just comes down to the fact that the team is better than everybody else.

People say that going to play in the Smith Center, the home of the University of North Carolina Tarheels, is hard.

It's really not hard to play there. It's hard to win there. Why? Because their teams are good. It's not because of the fans. It's not because the arena is the biggest in the league. It's because their teams are good. It's hard to beat them anywhere. Winning generally comes down to the strength of the team that you are playing versus the strength of your team. It's who plays better on that particular night.

T he home court advantage is less a factor now than it used to be. Teams are learning to play on the road more. They are getting more comfortable. I don't know what the statistics say—certainly you win more at home than you do away—but playing on your home court seems to be less of a factor.

The more times you go to a place, the more comfortable you should be there. Being smart in planning—how the team is going to travel; whether or not you are going to have a curfew and, if so, how late it will be; and what your arrival time at the arena will be—makes a difference. Our players generally like to go and relax, spend the night, practice, have a nice meal, and sleep in the next morning.

Some coaches like to go to an away site the day before and spend the night, practice at the facility, and then play. Others feel that the less time spent away from home, the better, and want to go the day of the game. I expect I'm somewhere in the middle. I don't want to spend too much time at a game site, because you get bored or restless. Yet I don't want to feel rushed either. I don't want to go somewhere and feel as if we've got to have our uniforms on as we're getting off the bus or plane.

T he Xs and Os of any sport are important. You've got to have an understanding of what you are trying to teach and how to put it all together. As a player, you have to be able to execute, but as a coach, you have to be grounded in all the fundamentals as well as able to develop a game strategy. You have to know your team and your opponents and plan accordingly.

Young coaches are probably more prepared in that sense than was my generation of coaches. They've been exposed to so much more. Television analysts, newspaper columnists, and recruiting newletters are all informative sources and seem to critique everything that we do. Although my generation watched basketball games on television when we were growing up, we didn't have someone as knowledgeable as Billy Packer analyzing the game.

The sheer number of basketball games available on television now is overwhelming. During the season, if you have cable television or a satellite dish, you can fill almost every waking hour watching games or replays of games.

S o much in basketball depends upon opportunities. In Tim Duncan's case, he had the door of opportunity opened early. When he came to Wake Forest, there was a huge need for his skills and his personality in our program, and we put him to work early. He quickly got on an incline that he stayed on throughout his four years.

He was constantly developing his skills and improving. Certainly, there were plateau periods in his development when he might reach a certain level and stay there for a few weeks before moving up to the next level. But he always kept getting better.

If the door of opportunity opens early for him as a professional, it will enhance his chances of being an impact rookie and will make him a better player three or four years down the road.

Tim was taught to be a low-post player. He feels very comfortable with his back to the basket. My philosophy is that a player starts inside and earns his way outside. If you do it the other way, you'll never get them to feel comfortable inside. If you have a room full of seven-foot players together and you say, "Any of you guys like to play inside?" you're going to have a very small percentage of them saying "yes."

Almost everybody wants to be something they're not. But in Tim Duncan's case, he's not afraid to be a tall center. That's what he's been all his life. Does that mean that he doesn't like to face the basket and shoot jumpers or put the ball on the floor and make plays? No. He likes to do that, but he earned his right to sometimes play outside here at Wake Forest. We didn't start him out there.

The nice thing about Tim was that he came here with few bad habits, basically because he had never formally been coached. As a youngster, Tim was coached by his brother-in-law, Rick Lowery. The high school athletic programs in St. Croix were somewhat unstructured when Tim was in school, thus he came to us eager to learn and physically ready to go.

Since he came here with few bad habits, the coaching that he was exposed to had a greater impact than it would have on most players who have come up through the domestic ranks—junior high, high school, AAU, and in some cases, junior college. These players have often been exposed to two or three different styles of coaching. They tend to be either entrenched in a certain way of doing things or they're mixed up because they've been exposed to so much. With Tim Duncan, we had a guy who was raw, but very talented.

I think Tim is more comfortable with his back to the basket than David Robinson was in college. David is something of a "tweener." I really don't know whether he's a center or a forward—but he's great at both.

Both Tim and David have a real passion for the game, which is invaluable for any player—and absolutely necessary if one is to be a great player. Another trait that will make them very successful is that they put themselves a distant second to the good of the team. I think they are both very selfless. I don't know David that well, but I know Tim, and he really thinks about the team much more than he does about himself.

F rom a physical standpoint, a good team is one that has a good low-post center as its backbone and a strong, versatile point guard as its head. On either side you need to have two good wings—one who can play off the dribble and the other who can shoot the ball with range. Hopefully, both have some playmaking abilities. Your fifth starter should be the player who best complements the strengths and minimizes the weaknesses of the other four. Some coaches might call this person the consummate role player. Perhaps the best recent example on one of my teams would be the role filled by Marc Blucas.

M ost coaches consider themselves to be either offensively or defensively more proficient. We all gravitate toward the things that we enjoy the most, and then we become good at those things. I think the enjoyment comes before the mastery.

From my viewpoint, it's easier to control a game defensively than it is offensively. If you can't control a game defensively—if you allow the other teams to take liberties with you—it becomes very difficult to win on a regular basis.

When I'm preparing our team to play another team, I first think, "How can we stop them? What do we have to do to stop them?" Then I work from there. Good defense keeps you from losing a game, then good offense can win it for you.

R epetition and doing things at close to game speed under close to game conditions are the best ways to learn in practice. For a coach, repetition is an invaluable teaching tool. Having your players practice something over and over and over, until they can almost effortlessly execute a technique or a set play, leads to confidence in game situations. The best learning occurs during game action. That's where you learn the most because you have the total impact of the experience.

M uscle memory still varies tremendously at this level. Some kids are ready to go the minute they pick up a ball, but it takes others half an hour to warm up. Some people's muscles learn more quickly than others, just like their brains. It's a matter of maturing at different times.

M any of the basic drills have remained the same during my years of teaching. We all tend to go back to doing things that we feel comfortable doing and that we know are proven over the course of time. The danger in continuing to do them the same way is boredom, which leads to slippage. If you have a player for four years at the collegiate level, you must work very hard to keep him alert and eager to improve.

It behooves a coach to constantly look for new and better ways to teach the game. If you can do that, you not only succeed from a teaching standpoint, but you also lessen the chance that boredom will set in.

You want to keep challenging your players and yourself in new and different ways. That's what coaching clinics are for. Coaches go and listen to other coaches talk and discuss new techniques and innovations—and that's important. A fellow coach once told me that if he came back from a clinic or conference with just *one* new idea or method, he considered it worthwhile.

A ll teams are going to have a routine for preparing for a game. It may differ slightly depending on whether you're home or away, but it will be pretty much the same. If we have two days to get ready for a game, that means we'll have two "on the court" preparations.

We'll usually show our team a 10 to 14-minute highlight tape of our opponent. That's all the film of the other team that they look at, but we usually show it twice. The night before the game, if we're home, we usually bring the team in around ten o'clock at night and shoot free throws and walk through things again defensively — and offensively if we need to.

Then, on the day of the game, we'll have a short shoot-around where we walk through everything — the whole game, really. Right before the game, we do it on the board. And then we play. So there are five or six different opportunities to prepare for the game.

What we try *not* to do is become too consumed with the other team, but at times we do that. We become too concerned about what the other team is doing and not concerned enough about what we're doing. There needs to be some balance.

I'm usually brain dead when games are over, so I try to get away. I don't want to rehash the game at that point. I want to go home and be with my family and be away from it for the night.

I try to watch films and review the game the next day. We make an 8 to 10-minute highlight/low-light tape for almost every game and have the team watch it. We might bring individuals back into the office to watch themselves, but time is a factor. We just don't have enough time to do as much film watching as we would like. We try to condense it as much as we can and still get the job done.

There's certainly value in watching yourself play. Sometimes you think you are doing one thing, but when you watch the tapes you realize, "That's not what I thought I did" or "Gosh, I didn't do that." You view yourself differently once you *actually* see yourself, and there's value to that.

O fficiating has improved over the years. Like coaches, officials are guardians of the game, and by and large they are becoming more accountable to themselves and to the game every year.

They attend self-improvement clinics and camps, and they're accountable to league supervisors, to coaches, to players, and to the game itself. Just like coaches, however, they first must be accountable to themselves, and I think they do a pretty good job of that.

W e did have two unfortunate situations in 1997 and both were very difficult to accept... Both games occurred in our coliseum against conference teams — Maryland and North Carolina State. The outcomes of both games were greatly affected by what were proven to be incorrect calls that went against Wake Forest, and we lost both games.

With the score tied, a Maryland player made a last-second shot that was ruled good at the buzzer. Upon later review using television replays, it was clear that the shot had been released after the horn had sounded and should not have counted. The game, which should have gone into overtime, was won by Maryland in regulation.

In the game with North Carolina State, a Wolfpack player took a last-second shot which was credited as a 3-point goal. Again, television replays showed an erroneous call, because it was clear that the player's feet were on the line, and the shot should only have counted as a 2-point shot. Instead of Wake Forest winning by 1 point, the game went into overtime, which we lost.

Coupled with a incorrect call that enabled Duke to beat Virginia, these games meant that there was a potential three-game swing in the conference race. We had two losses in games we could have won, and Duke got a win in a game they could have lost.

Once things like that happen, if you allow yourself to focus on them, they're going to continue to eat at you. It goes back to the question of what can you do about something after it happens. You try to use situations like those to strengthen you, but I'm not sure we ever got to that point. We tried to use them as a catalyst—a springboard toward toughness.

As far as using instant replay, you should be able to check certain situations that involve the score or the clock. You ought to be able to double-check end-of-game situations when there's a question such as, "Did the horn go off before the shot?" I think we will eventually get to that point, because if a replay offers proof beyond a reasonable doubt, then it ought to be accepted. So much effort and emotion goes into each game that you can't afford to let a wrong stand.

I'm not sure that we need to go a lot further than that or we'd be challenging whistles every time they blow. Things that require judgment must be left to the officials. Their judgments have to be final. Their decisions have to be final.

Situations like the two we had in 1997 are really hard on a team. My players were looking at me to, "Fix it, fix it." And you can't. Once a game becomes official, you can't go back and change it.

Players work so hard and put so much of themselves on the line in basketball. They practice hard, they play hard, and they root hard for each other. There's so much at stake — and when a game is decided by a referee's whistle at the end, it becomes difficult to accept. The players have got to blame somebody. They blame the official, but he's not going to talk to them. So they look to the coach to "make it right," and when you can't, that becomes hard to deal with.

T he lines of communication between coaches and officials have gotten better. We're more comfortable with each other now. One of the worst things that can happen from an officiating and coaching standpoint is that the relationship becomes adversarial. You don't want coaches and officials to look at each other with an "us versus them" mentality. If it gets to that point, it can get ugly and can be very uncomfortable, and the game suffers.

Most coaches and officials feel more comfortable with clear lines of communication. We're all human beings and, by working together, we can make the game better. I think that's in the process of happening even as we prepare for another year.

T he women's professional basketball leagues are going to survive and should eventually do well. The new WNBA surpassed all expectations in its first summer and the ABL may have more actual talent. But there are some things that women's basketball could do that would help the game. If women continue to play with a 10-foot basket, I don't think they're ever going to really be able to play above the rim, which is one of the exciting things about basketball.

If the basket was lowered to 9½ feet, for instance, then, all of a sudden, some of the women are up around the rim and you'll see more dunking. Six inches is not going to make any difference for the spectators. Just the thrill of seeing women jump like that would be exciting.

Women play with a smaller ball that is easier to handle, so why not lower the basket so they can get to it more easily? I don't see anything wrong with that. Anything that improves the game should be done.

About 17 years ago, the owners of the Five-Star Camp came to me and said they'd like to expand it into the girls' arena and open two camps—one in the north and one in the south—and that they'd like for me to operate the one in the south. Rick Pitino agreed to run the one in the north.

I looked at the opportunity as good for me from two standpoints. One, I wanted to operate it as a family camp. I wanted my wife to act as a kind of den mother for the girls. She had never had a daughter of her own and I thought she would be very good with the campers. She *is* very good with them and has proven to be a big hit. I also wanted her to handle the financial and administrative end of things.

The other appealing aspect was the chance to get the whole family together for a week of camp. I thought it would be fun, and we've done it every summer since. It gives us a chance to have a family reunion of sorts. For seven years we had one week of camp each summer. Then, about ten years ago, we added a second week. Because of all my other commitments now, we may go back to just one week a summer.

At the time we began the girls' camp, I was an assistant coach and every bit of money I could make was important to me. That camp really sent both of my boys to college. So it's been good for me in every single way.

I've been amazed at the thirst for knowledge that every female camper has had. The girls really want to learn. You can teach a certain amount at boys' camps, but the boys grow tired of the teaching and want to play. The boys' attitude is, "Put me five on five out there and let me go. Let me show you what I can do."

But the girls really want to be taught. They want to learn about pivoting and rebounding and blocking out. They want to know how to shoot a jump shot and the correct way to handle the ball. They want the science of the game. Basically, we use the same format as we do in the boys camp, but without as much emphasis on the best players.

There is no question that the girls' skill levels have improved over the years. Right now they shoot as well as boys, though not off the move. If they get two feet up under them, they can really shoot the basketball well. It's been fun for us to watch the growth of girls' basketball, because I only get to coach them for one week or two a year.

Much as we've been able to follow the boys I coached in high school or college, we've followed our female campers as they have gone on to college basketball and now into professional basketball.

The girl who made the very first basket in the new WNBA had been one of our campers. That was a great experience for us and I took a lot of pride in that, because I remember the year she was at the camp as a rising high school senior, she was one of the top five girls in her class nationally.

We accept girls from the eighth through the twelfth grades and we're not concerned with their level of play. We really are a teaching camp, and the first priority is for us to teach. We want the campers leaving camp the last day saying, "I'm glad I came. I learned a lot. I'm going home tired but it's been really good."

It's an interesting situation, but we haven't been very successful getting women to work as coaches at the camp. We might get one or two a week, but female high school coaches seem tied to the mentality of teaching nine months and taking three months off. Family responsibilities may be a factor, as well as the fact that for many of them, their income is the family's second, whereas male coaches may be their families' sole providers and for them, the extra money is important.

Not only would having more women as coaches increase our network, but even more importantly, it would be good from a safety standpoint. In our world of excessive litigation, you can't be too careful. We feel a real need to get more women involved, but we just haven't been able to do it.

Running a camp is very demanding. The responsibility of 24 hours a day is hard. But it's worth it because the girls have done well and they really put a lot of effort into improving their games.

T he majority of coaches are givers who share their knowledge and their experience. They know that there are very few secrets in the game and, by and large, they do a good job of helping each other. That's one of the special things about coaching.

Coaching clinics are very popular right now. I've just made a videotape that will be available nationally. There may be a conflict between revealing what I know to my opponents and sharing what I know with my colleagues. But I'm not afraid that the video will "expose my secrets" or anything like that. Games still come down to execution. Theoretically knowing something is one thing; being able to execute it with five specific players, under pressure, and under the lights is another.

T he game of basketball was given to us by James Naismith and all the others who played and coached through the years. When those of my generation began coaching, we accepted responsibility for the game, and now it's our obligation to make it better for those following us, like my sons and others in their generation.

One of the ways you do that is by sharing ideas. Don't be afraid. Share what you've learned, for others will share with you. The truth is, there are very few secrets in the game—and if they are secret now, they won't be for long!

# Afterword

# A Day in the Life . . .*

8:00 a.m.    Went over correspondence; schedule for the day, etc.

9:00 a.m.    Interview with Winston-Salem *Journal* sportswriter
             *(interrupted by three phone calls; one a telephone interview about Tim Duncan for a San Antonio newspaper)*

9:30 a.m.    Met with "Mr. Smith" and son
             *(father wanted me to talk with his son, a former straight-A student, who has become so consumed with basketball that his grades had fallen dramatically. "Johnny" had been one of our summer campers and "Mr. Smith" thought I have some influence. "Johnny" and I agreed that "Johnny" would write to me weekly about how things were going.)*

---

* This day, while not untypical, was compiled from several different days on my calendar. On any given day, I may also have: meetings with players; ex-players stopping by to chat; administrative details to deal with; the taping of a television interview; the shooting of a commercial for Wake Forest basketball; talks with athletic administration staff; or numerous media requests for "the inside scoop." A coach's life is fast-paced (not just on the court), varied, demanding, and rarely dull!

| | |
|---|---|
| 10:00 a.m. | Discussed bids for bus contract for transporting team; inspected one of the new bus models |
| 10:30 a.m. | Mr. Duncan, Tim's father called, just to keep in touch; I signed off on travel expenses; went over practice schedule for the next week; had a call from the National Association of Basketball Coaches Congress; watched tape with Loren Woods |
| 11:00 a.m. | Weekly ACC coaches' teleconference |
| 12:45 p.m. | Went to run |
| 1:45 p.m. | Grabbed a bite as I prepared for staff meeting |
| 2:00 p.m. | Staff meeting with assistant coaches to discuss practice |
| 3:30 p.m. | Two-hour team practice<br>*(time varies from day to day and from week to week depending on the players' class schedules and their day off)* |
| 7:00 p.m. | Speaking engagement with Screamin' Demons student support group<br>*(at least this one was in town; last week I went to Blacksburg, Virginia to speak at the VPI Tip-Off Banquet)* |
| 10:00 p.m. | Got home; have book proofs to go over |

# A Year in the Life ...

July:             Begin recruiting on the road, summer camps

August:           End of summer school, chance for coaches' vacations, begin fall semester

September:        Recruiting, preseason conditioning for players, settle players' academic schedules

October:          Finish preseason conditioning, begin official practice, continue with recruiting and official campus visits of prospects

November:         Early signing of National Letters of Intent, exhibition games and regular season games begin

December:         Regular season games continue, break for exams and Christmas

January &
February:         Conference games

March:            March Madness

April:            Final Four and National Association of Basketball Coaches convention, speaking to alumni groups, coaches' clinics, and preparing for summer camps

May:              Speaking to alumni groups, ACC meetings, final preparations for summer camps

June:             Summer camps

July:             Cycle begins anew